Will You Worship?

God's Invitation to a Transforming Life

Ray Jones

With Dino Senesi

30 Day Journal and Small Group Gatherings

Foreword by Robert Emmitt, Community Bible Church
San Antonio, Texas

xulon PRESS

Will You Worship?
God's Invitation to a Transforming Life
by Ray Jones with Dino Senesi

Printed in the United States of America

ISBN 9781619047709

www.xulonpress.com

The next 30 days could change your life! You are about to go on a journey far beyond knowing about God, to the actual KNOWING of our awesome, beautiful, wonderful, knowable God! As one who longs to see people go beyond mere head knowledge of God to a personal, life altering relationship with God, I highly recommend 'Will You Worship?' Ray Jones is a man after God's own heart.
Tommy Walker - Worship Leader and Songwriter
Christian Assembly – Los Angeles

'Will You Worship?' by Ray Jones and Dino Senesi takes the participant on the journey of experiencing and rediscovering worship. They approach worship holistically, seeing our connection with God as the source of our transformation and sending. Engage in the exercises and questions at the end of each session on your own or with a friend, but don't skip them!
Bob Logan - Author of Making Life Count and Coaching 101
Logan Leadership

Not only is 'Will you Worship?' an amazing personal devotional for any leader, it should be used as a small group or worship team devotional as well. Ray Jones has mentored hundreds of leaders over the years. This 30-day journey will better equip our future leaders as well as us seasoned vets.
Phil Sillas - Song Discovery A&R Director
Worship Leader Magazine

We can't participate fully in God's mission for us without the gifts of worship to sustain and transform us. Ray and Dino remind us of these truths. They teach us that worship is an invitation to a transformed life that blesses others. This experience of 30 days will fast forward your missional engagement personally and as a congregation.
Reggie McNeal - Author of Work of Heart and Missional Renaissance
Leadership Network

I will read after anyone whose pivotal passion is to pursue the presence of God. That is where I want to preside!

Jack Taylor – Author of *The Hallelujah Factor* and President
Dimensions Ministries

'Will You Worship?' is a great tool to daily center your heart on Christ and what He has done for you. To place yourself in His presence is to position yourself in a posture primed for transformation. Thirty meetings with God is a step in the right direction for any serious Christ-follower.

Eric Geiger - Author of *Simple Church*
VP Lifeway Christian Resources

Invitation, transformation, sending. Intimacy with God changes us and compels us into His mission. May God use this worship journal to deepen believers for Kingdom advancing change.

Chris Beard – Lead Pastor
First Christian Assembly of God Cincinnati

Table of Contents

Foreword

O ne of my first true worship experiences came in 1990 while listening to a cassette tape on cheap headphones. I was on the mission field in Costa Rica listening to music and trying to fall asleep. I wasn't looking for a worship experience when the song "Give Thanks" began to play. The Lord touched my heart, soul, mind and body through that one song. My eyes filled with tears as I played it over and over again. I had been a pastor for 13 years. I had always enjoyed the music and songs yet I had never truly worshiped through music, until that night. My prayer was *Lord, if you ever make me a pastor again, could we have this kind of music?*

My life has changed dramatically since then and I am still seeing God touch lives worldwide through worship. Community Bible Church (CBC) has sent cases of our worship CDs around the world. God has used them as a tool to touch people 24/7. Worship and God's mission go together. That is why I believe the *Will You Worship?* Project is timely and urgent. God's mission is to turn everyday people into worshipers and worshipers into missionaries. Worship is not a part of God's mission in the world—worship is God's mission.

When I met Ray Jones, we became friends instantly. When I asked him to lead worship at Community Bible Church, he asked me what I was looking for in a worship leader. I said someone who would lead us in worship and teach us how to worship. It was a divine appointment. Ray has led and taught CBC how to worship since 1992. He has shown individuals, families and groups how to worship Jesus. He has taught us to worship not just on Sunday, but on every day of the week.

The vision for this project is simple and remarkable. Imagine if God's people committed to worship God more consistently and passionately over a 30-day period. We would know God more intimately and become more like Jesus. People around us would see and crave the lives we were living. The good news is that God is inviting them to the same kind of life. Worshiping people being transformed by God become both an advertisement and an invitation! What amazing grace! In the next 30 days you will learn how to worship, but the question is in the title "Will You Worship?" I pray that you will. If you do, God will transform your life.

Robert Emmitt
Senior Pastor
Community Bible Church, San Antonio, Texas

Preface and Acknowledgements

Did you ever experience the euphoria of going on vacation with your family growing up? How exciting to go somewhere just for fun! I was a young child when our family made a trip to Canon City, Colorado to see Royal Gorge Bridge and Park (http://royal-gorgebridge.com/). What an amazing destination! All five of us piled in our old Impala and traveled for days. We lived in Springhill, Louisiana at the time, so it was over 1200 miles to Royal Gorge. I remember we would stop at roadside parks to make sandwiches on the long, low budget trip out west.

In spite of the fun, looking back, it was a small trip within a big journey. The big journey began in 1954 when I was born in Tulia, Texas at Swisher County Hospital. Included were my father (Raymond), mother (Mildred), and my two older sisters (Martha, Caren). Never once did I want to be on any other journey with anybody else. The short journey was about Colorado and the Royal Gorge on vacation and the big journey was about life. Most of you have similar memories.

God invited me on a lifelong and eternal journey with Him in 1960. The greatest joy in my life is the fact that He found me that day in Springhill, Louisiana and invited me to Him. At times I confess I am a bit mystified by all this and at the same time I am amazed. Why did He invite me? How did I know to say *yes*?

My journey has not been perfect. I have disappointed God many times during the journey. I also admit He has surprised me more than a few times. Yet I am honored to be a part of God's family and have enjoyed benefits beyond belief. Never once have I wanted to be on any other journey with anybody else.

Life with Jesus describes the everyday experience of a Christ-follower. The big journey includes 24 hour trips that can go anywhere. He invites me to a life of worship daily and I have a choice – I can say *yes* or I can say *no*. My negative response may sound something like, "No Lord, I am busy and stressed out. Thanks but no thanks for today. I am sure it would have been great." Every day I have a choice.

Many Christ-followers have connected on the big journey yet are missing the beauty, greatness, and potential of a daily love relationship with Him. I confess it's true at times in my life. I may have perfectly good reasons (in my mind) to say *no* to Jesus. And in spite of the fact that He knows it's a bad decision, He loves me anyway. At times I said *no* without realizing it and at other times I may have had a *mock quiet time* and ignored His presence in the process. It is like going to church externally and internally being in another place.

I wonder about the Royal Gorge trips I have missed on my spiritual journey. I wonder what joy, encouragement, and amazement I bypassed. I wonder how different I would be now – a better husband, father, son, brother, leader, and a deeper man of God.

So, what is the purpose of *Will You Worship?* God is inviting you to an authentic daily worship life. What if you committed to 30 days of intense, focused worship with your Savior? Would it matter? What would God do in and around you? How would your relationships change with family, friends, work associates, and even the unbelievers in your world?

The purpose of this journal is for you to go deeper (than ever before) with God. I am not inviting you to a mystical or intimidating place, but to a deeper and better place. Neither am I trying to make you feel guilty because you are not praying, singing, serving or reading enough chapters of the Bible each day. Nevertheless, if you have been leaving something out of your relationship with God that could make a dramatic difference, would you want to know? There are deeper places to go with God. Do you have the courage to go to where God is? Too often we ask Jesus Christ to follow us instead of following Him into the arms of the Father. Instead of saying, "Jesus, come to me," will you boldly draw near to Him?

If you decide to accept this mission, God will show you the time, place, and the actions to take. God will always give you what you need in order to do what He wants. We invite you on a great journey – a life-changing, community transforming, world-shaking journey with Jesus Christ the Son of the living God! Let's head to the Royal Gorge!

Acknowledgements

I want to thank Dino Senesi for being one of the men that has challenged me to a deeper walk with Christ. He is the one that would not let the vision of this book die. Thank you to my precious wife, Andrea, who has encouraged me and put up with me during the process of writing this book. Thanks to my awesome sons, David, Jonathan, Benjamin and Christopher who have heard this material so many times they could teach the material without me. My deepest gratitude is expressed to my dad (who is in heaven) and mom who put the desire to be a worshiper in my heart. I give thanks for my sisters Martha and Caren who have remained consistent in their walk with Christ and have encouraged me to do the same. And I thank the Lord for...

- Rodney Wood who poured his life into me at his breakfast table every Friday morning for over 2 years.
- My Pastor Robert Emmitt who has allowed me to serve with him for over 19 years.
- The Radiance Ministry supporters and board of directors; Ruben and Sandra Fechner; Bill and Janet Robertson.
- Tom Morgan who has mentored me in leadership and supported this effort.
- Valerie Johnson who has spent hours proofing, editing, and making great suggestions.
- All the gatherings and people who have listened and responded to the message of worship that God has been burning into my life over the last 40 years.
- Christ who loves me and redeemed me, the one for whom this book is written.

Ray Jones

Since our early morning New Orleans' discipleship meetings in 1983, Ray Jones has been one of the *Apostle Pauls* in my life. We memorized scripture, studied *Disciples are Made, Not Born* by Walt Henrichen, and preached in the streets of Mexico, El Salvador, and New Orleans. Ray and I have lived in community since those first meetings although we have never lived in the same city together for long. Yet we have walked together all over the world through incredible disappointments as well as epic wins.

I am honored to be a part of the *Will You Worship?* Project. I first heard Ray teach this material in the early '80s. It was not in print and was never intended to be until now. The purpose of the *Will You Worship?* Project is to address a reality: *Many who say "Yes!" to the big eternal journey with Jesus never fully embrace Him daily as a worshiper.*

We can only speculate what we are missing when a *Come in, sit down, and do life with Jesus* daily worship journey is overlooked. Our friends, communities, and nations wait to see lives authentically shaped by Jesus. May they see power of the resurrected Jesus flow through our lives to change the world: "That I may know Him and the power of His resurrection and the fellowship of His sufferings, being conformed to His death" (Philippians 3:10).

Treat each day's assignment like an exit from your routine essential to the success of your journey with Jesus. As you exit look for things that will help you get refueled and refreshed. Answer every question, write every prayer, and read every scripture. Then get moving again! The Royal Gorge awaits you!

Acknowledgements

My incredible wife, Yvette; My wonderful daughters, Krista, Anna, and Abby; My super son-in-law, David; and my awesome grandsons, Brock and Owen, are all God's greatest blessings in my life.

Every church home on my journey has been a gift from God: Grace Baptist, First Baptist Kenner, First Baptist Marrero, Liberty Heights, Willow Ridge, The River (Pine Tree Hill), and North Rock Hill.

God has used countless people to pour into my life. Special thanks to those who were direct contributors to this project: Dan Barringer, Kay Carver, John Donovan, Emmet Foxworth, Wes Gardner, Michelle Harter, Joshua Hieber, Bryan Plyler, and Chris Ruppe.

Dino Senesi

The Next 30 Days
Where are You Going?

As the deer pants for the water brooks,
So my soul pants for You, O God.
My soul thirsts for God, for the living God;
When shall I come and appear before God?
(Psalm 42:1-2)

Approximately 6:30 a.m. in Moldova my apartment phone rang. I rushed to answer hoping it was a call from home. When I answered my wife, Andrea, simply said, "There is someone here that wants to talk to you." My three-year old son, Christopher, got on the line and said, "I want you, right now!"

When I told him that it would be five more days until I would be home, he broke out into a heart wrenching sob. Wow! I felt terrible. Andrea calmed him after a few minutes by convincing him to make a plan to count down the days until my return.

I went to teach at the seminary that day with a broken heart. I wanted to go home immediately to be with my son. As I prayed with some of the teachers that morning one of them prayed, "Lord, may my heart long for you like Christopher longs for his Daddy." At that moment reality struck me in the face. How often do I long for my heavenly Father with the same passion that Christopher longed for me? Over the next 30 days I hope you will become more familiar with God through worship and establish a place with Him that you long to revisit. Once you get there, nothing can replace your personal connection with Him.

We all have a thirst for a close connection to God, our Father, but we often ignore it. Our thirst is God's invitation to a deeper relationship with Him. I like the way *The Message* Bible paraphrases Paul's words to the Romans:

This resurrection life you received from God is not a timid, grave-tending life. It's adventurously expectant, greeting God with a childlike 'What's next, Papa?' God's

Spirit touches our spirits and confirms who we really are. We know who he is, and we know who we are: Father and children. And we know we are going to get what's coming to us—an unbelievable inheritance! We go through exactly what Christ goes through. If we go through the hard times with him, then we're certainly going to go through the good times with him! (Romans 8:15-17 MSG)

I learned three unforgettable lessons about God from my conversation with Christopher. As you begin this 30-day worship journey with God, the lessons provide a great place to start. In them you will find perspectives that will help you get the most out of your relationship with God, your heavenly Father.

Thirst for God

First, *when life doesn't go our way, we become more open to a deeper life with God.* One of my favorite preachers, Ron Dunn, said something I will never forget. Sadly, it described my own experience and most of you are probably like me. He said, "A man will never trust God until he has to."

There is something miraculously encoded in our spiritual DNA to thirst for God, yet our pride sends us searching for other ways to fill our need. The challenges and stressors of life will make us thirsty for God but will not automatically drive us to God. God never seems to be our default mode. A fresh, daily relationship with the living water, Jesus Christ, is the only way to be satisfied. Without an authentic, daily relationship with Jesus even the kindest, most religious people will remain thirsty.

The psalmist painted an unforgettable picture to illustrate our God-dependence: "As the deer pants for the water brooks, So my soul pants for You, O God" (Psalm 42:1). Something about the panting, restless deer connected to his soul. Only one thing would bring rest and comfort to the thirsty deer – a drink of fresh water. The psalmist referred back to a day when God was much more real to him. He was looking for a God he already knew was missing. Like the deer, he was nervous, restless, and searching. Nothing would satisfy him except the God he had experienced in the past.

The reality is, most of us live in a constant state of *circumstances beyond our control* and we don't like living that way. My son, Christopher, wanted something that he could not have, that no toy, game, or snack could give. Nothing else would do, but a connection with his dad.

Like the thirsty deer in Psalm 42:1, you will go frantically searching for relief from God as life gets difficult. Over these next 30 days, I hope the journey you walk with God will become more intimate, familiar, comfortable and safe to you. I pray that the selfish pride that assumes you can handle life without God will disappear as you embrace a more intimate relationship with Him.

God Cares for You

The next lesson is that *we are God's children and our Father is sympathetic to our need*. He promises He will provide your every need. What you think you need is not always what you need. That is your Father's call. He is the loving and wise Father, who is at work making us become all He has planned for us in conforming us to Christ. He knows best and as worshipers, we commit ourselves to His care.

Be encouraged by these realities:
- God the Father cares when you hurt.
- God the Son cares when your marriage is not working or when you lose your job.
- God the Spirit understands your deepest fears and knows your greatest temptations.

Be assured as God's child that anything you are missing from Him is not because He is out of touch or taking care of greater concerns. He is in your world and as you grow deeper with Him, you will trust His decisions. Trusting Christ results in incredible freedom and peace regardless of what negative situations surround you. Notice this powerful explanation:

Now that we know what we have—Jesus, this great High Priest with ready access to God—let's not let it slip through our fingers. We don't have a priest who is out of touch with our reality. He's been through weakness and testing, experienced it all—all but the sin. So let's walk right up to him and get what he is so ready to give. Take the mercy, accept the help. (Hebrews 4:14-16 MSG)

I was sad that I could not meet Christopher's immediate need, but it made me feel loved and important that he wanted to be with me so badly. I know that as his father I can never do for him what God can. But I can relate to the challenges of fatherhood. At times we want God our Father to give us a better life with no strings attached. Deeper life with Him comes when we thirst to be with Him with no agenda and we know by faith, that he will never disappoint us.

How it must please our Father when we can sincerely say what the psalmist said, "My soul longed and even yearned for the courts of the LORD; My heart and my flesh sing for joy to the living God" (Psalm 84:2). When we move from individual worship into a corporate worship gathering — the bigger dream of a movement of God becomes even more apparent. The starting place of all worship is birthed when His children are incredibly satisfied with Him, alone!

Your Journey with Jesus

The final lesson I needed was that *my desire for quick results in my relationship with God hurts progress.* Once I embrace my need for a relationship with God then the rest is His responsibility. My human nature causes me to feel entitled to fast response times and instant results from God with personal satisfaction guaranteed. The simple just got really complicated, don't you think? My son wanted me home *now*! Yet there were perfectly good reasons why things did not turn out the way he wanted.

View the next 30 days as an incredibly valuable next step on your journey with Jesus, not a quick fix for everything you don't like about your life. The pace of life is so much faster than 50 years ago. Faster computers, state of the art smart phones, and fast food delivered to our homes in 30 minutes guaranteed has raised our expectations of how life should work. But life with God is a lifelong journey that some people miss because it just doesn't happen fast enough. They run their own race (a sprint) instead of God's race (a marathon). Look at this incredible word from God:

> So then, my beloved, just as you have always obeyed, not as in my presence only, but now much more in my absence, work out your salvation with fear and trembling; for it is God who is at work in you, both to will and to work for His good pleasure. (Philippians 2:12-13)

Memorize this verse. Post it on your bathroom mirror and car dashboard. Even better go Old Testament and plaster it on your forehead! Going deeper with God is an incredible journey **worked out** over a lifetime. But even greater, God is **at work in you** for all that time! We have hope because He grows us deeper. The responsibility to grow in Christ is not left up to us alone.

Defining Moments

Your life will consist of defining moments that change everything. Some of these moments are painful while others will be remembered as great wins. God is inviting you into an intimate love relationship with Him. The Creator of the universe is also the lover of your soul. What an incredible invitation! What a defining moment! He said, "Behold, I stand at the door and knock; if anyone hears My voice and opens the door, I will come in to him and will dine with him, and he with Me" (Rev. 3:20). A highly relational Savior wants to come in, sit down, and do life with you!

The setting, actors, and scripts are different on each person's journey with Jesus. The highs may be higher. The lows, unfortunately, may be lower. You have a role to play in your story, but the lead role rightfully belongs to *Jesus Christ . . . the same yesterday, today, and forever* (Hebrews 13:8). Christ makes us all new creations in Him—created and formed to have a love relationship with the God of the universe.

Will You Worship? God's Invitation to a Transforming Life (WYW) is about God's mission in the world. The project paints a picture of how God works in our lives and what He wants in the world. The Bible, from beginning to end, is about a relationship between God and people. Worship initiatives often focus on the experiential side of worship with no grasp of God's purposes. Jesus did not come to give us a mystical, feel good experience designed around our musical preferences. Jesus came to invite people into relationship with Him and thus, change the world. He came to change invitees into inviters on His behalf!

Three defining moments fuel what God wants in the world and how He works:

1. **Invitation.** The first defining moment is the ***invitation***. Jesus invites you to know and worship Him. Thus, you get the title for the project, *Will You Worship?* Deeper life with God is often what believers want, but they believe Bible knowledge is all that is required. Knowing more will never mature people without personal surrender to the God of the universe. When Jesus invites you into this relationship your response to His invitation is the next step. The desired response is complete abandonment and surrender to Him. "Now on the last day, the great day of the feast, Jesus stood and cried out, saying, 'If anyone is thirsty, let him come to Me and drink'" (John 7:37).

2. **Transformation.** The second defining moment is ***transformation.*** Jesus transforms those who worship Him. You cannot live in the presence of God without being radically changed. The second element involves implementation of a new and better approach to life empowered by Jesus Christ. Here you see yourself as a deeper worshiper of Jesus Christ. Your view of who He is, how He works, and what He wants evolves. Your reply to His purpose is to embrace His change, enjoy His work, and become a new person. "And do not be conformed to this world, but be transformed by the renewing of your mind, so that you may prove what the will of God is, that which is good and acceptable and perfect" (Rom. 12:2).

3. **Sending.** The final defining moment is ***sending***. Jesus now sends you across the street and around the world to invite other people to know Him. You serve and give to communicate the love of Jesus Christ in a tangible way (Mark 10:45). You care about the people who live on the margins of life. You engage life with Jesus as a missionary inviting people and being an invitation to the Christ life. Like the prophet Isaiah (Isaiah 6:8), you respond to God with a *send me* answer. Your life as a worshiper is defined by obedience, love, and service.

God will always change true worshipers into missionaries. Worship is not the end but the beginning. You now become a living invitation from Jesus to the people in your world. Then the cycle starts again with them as God changes people far from Him into transformed missionaries. Their lives become living invitations to Jesus for everyone in their world. We call that multiplication; when multiplication happens fast, we call that a movement of God.

Jesus, as the lead architect of your life, will then build patterns of mission, mentoring, and follow through into your life. You are not living an inspired life you are living a life empowered by God's Spirit. The third defining moment involves a permanent life-long approach to finishing well as a missionary. You are transformed and then become an instrument of transformation in the world. "So Jesus said to them again, 'Peace be with you; as the Father has sent Me, I also send you'" (John 20:21).

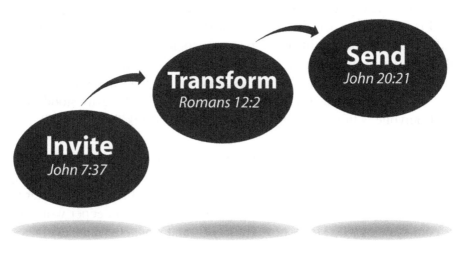

How God Works

Why 30 Days?

Experts have varying opinions on how long it takes to develop a habit. But in the Bible we learn of even greater potential in time set aside for God. In the first chapter of Acts, 120 believers went to the upper room. For 10 days they focused their attention on God and look at what happened. They were equipped and empowered by the Holy Spirit to become instruments to change the world. After they left the room, Pentecost happened, the Holy Spirit came to stay and 3,000 people (at least) came to faith in Christ. The church exploded. Why? A group of people intentionally went before the Lord for a period of time. The presence of God transformed lives. Invitees became missionaries and inviters. Intentional periods of seeking God have extraordinary potential to expand the Kingdom of God.

The Will You Worship? (WYW) Vision - 30 days of deeper worship was birthed from a passion to see a movement of God. We see thousands of churches and hundreds of thousands of believers experiencing a new passion for God resulting in a new level of transformation. Millions of people in America could be impacted by Christians living in the presence of God daily. Believers would then move beyond God as a great idea to daily interaction with a God whom they could experience. The psalmist declared, "Taste and see that the LORD is good. How happy is the man who takes refuge in Him!" (Psalm 34:8).

The WYW Mission - Over the next five weeks you will have 30 meetings with God. By investing 30 minutes each meeting you can pray, read scripture, journal and be coached through a process of going deeper with God. Invest thought and prayer in every coaching question. You may need more space to write than provided. God is building something deeper in you. Give Him space to work. We highly recommend you enlist a prayer partner or team to pray that God would do a deeper work in you. Give them updates on the process to keep them praying. Accountability is critical to change and growth.

Your local church or small group could create a great environment where a group of people can walk through *WYW* together. You can also get a friend to walk through the journal so you can pray and debrief together. Walking through this process with friends will be a great help. You can hold each other accountable and share encouraging stories about what God is doing.

Before you begin, access your calendar and plan the next five weeks. *Pray.* Schedule your 30-minute *WYW* meetings with God for 30 days. You have a makeup day each week. Look for obstacles and challenges and plan around them. Answer three key questions at the end of this section.

Although the same time and place every day is often best, there may be days that require moving your meetings with God around. Focus and intentionality will be elements God uses to help you go deeper. We know it will be a challenge. But if you choose to go on this journey God will provide what you need to get it done. God will give you time to do what He wants.

Imagine what would happen in the next five weeks if you focused on worshiping God? How would your life be different? What kind of impact would it have in your family, home, workplace, and church? We invite you on an incredible, life-changing, community transforming, world shaking journey with Jesus Christ, the Son of the living God! Let's go on this mission together to see what God has planned!

Complete the coaching questions below before you begin your 30-day journey. God will use the questions to help you plan the next steps to investing all of yourself into the process!

What changes are needed to create space for meetings with God (Give God Space)?

_____

_____

_____

Who do I need to tell about these changes and my commitment (My Prayer Team)?

_____

_____

_____

Who/What can help me finish well (Keys to Success)?

_____

_____

_____

DAY 1 – WHERE HAVE YOU BEEN?

And now, Israel, what does the LORD your God require from you, but to fear the LORD your God, to walk in all His ways and love Him, and to serve the LORD your God with all your heart and with all your soul.
(Deuteronomy 10:12)

I grew up in a Christian home and was blessed to be surrounded by godly people. My story is similar to Pastor Timothy's from the Bible, "and that from childhood you have known the sacred writings which are able to give you the wisdom that leads to salvation through faith which is in Christ Jesus" (2 Timothy 3:15). My family taught me about Jesus from my birth. My salvation experience came when I was six years old, and I have never really gotten over it.

I sensed a calling from God to ministry when I was 14 years old. That experience was real, changing the course of my life forever. The most incredible life you could ever lead is a life that is continually pursuing what the Lord has for you. Though I have failed Him many times, He has always loved and pursued me. Watching God at work in my life created a desire in me to follow and serve Him. Like most of you, I wonder how He puts up with me, but in reality God has shown me love, grace and mercy for all of my life.

My dad was known as a *Minister of Music* back in the day. Now we call them "worship leaders" or "worship pastors." My mother was the organist at the church where Dad served. I was sitting on the organ bench before I was born. I learned my passion for openly expressing my love for Christ from my parents. They played and sang with passion. Styles of worship and song lists change, but worship will always be an issue of the heart.

My parents were passionate worshipers beyond Sunday morning church services. When I was a kid, we had one radio station we could pick up in our old Plymouth. Most of the time, we provided our own entertainment. As we traveled to church meetings we would sing wonderful worship songs. There was so much joy and for me it was just plain fun! We sang many of the old spirituals and choruses that you may have never heard like, *Everybody Ought to Know Who Jesus Is*.

We had the greatest time praising God. I would often ask, "What do you think God thought about that last song?" Someone would always say, "I think God liked it." Then we'd go into the church, and it was like God died and no one bothered to tell us! Have you ever been to that church? I call it: *First Church of the Frigidaire*. The reality and joy of what happened in our old car on the way to church did not seem to be the same reality of what was happening in church. How can expressing your love to the God, who delivered you from your sin, be so cold and lifeless?

My Worship Journey

I was bothered by this contradiction as I began to lead worship in churches. What was real? What happened in our old Plymouth or what happened when we got to church? I was taught that as a worship leader my job was to prepare people for the main event, the sermon. So that's just what I did. I was a great setup guy. However, deep in my heart I found myself empty. I knew there had to be more than what I was experiencing as a worship leader. I thought to myself, "You know, if this is it, I am not sure I want to spend my life doing this gig."

I asked the Lord to show me what was making me so restless. His answer was life-changing, "Ray, you're not really worshiping me." You thought I was going to blame someone else, didn't you? God is like that with me. The truth was that I was the problem. He showed me I was getting people to relate to me and each other, but I wasn't getting them to relate to Him.

So I began a new journey as a true worshiper. Truthfully, you cannot lead people to a place that you have never been before. To lead worship, you must first be a worshiper yourself and then invite people to follow you.

God mentored me through a process of capturing His heart about true worship. He issued the most incredible invitation since the day He first invited me to follow Him. Jesus the Christ, the Messiah, had invited me to worship Him! From that day to this, He has continued to teach me about worship. Many of the lessons I've learned will be unpacked over the days to come in hopes that they can help you. I hope you can move farther and faster in your relationship with God than I did.

My whole perspective about worship has changed as has my view of God. (Funny, how those two are connected). My God is great and there is plenty more of Him to know and experience. My worship journey continues even as I write this journal. God's grace and mercy for me is *new every morning* (Lamentations 3:22-23). Where have you been so far on your worship journey? How will that influence where you need to go? Will you join me over the next 30 days?

Debrief with God - *Read Deuteronomy 10*

- How did your first worship experiences influence you?

_____

_____

_____

- When does God seem the most real to you now?

_____

_____

_____

- Where do you struggle the most in personal worship?

_____

_____

_____

- What would you like your personal worship life to look like 30 days from now?

_____

_____

_____

- What is one step you can make for your vision to become a reality?

_____

_____

_____

- How can you express what God has said in a prayer to Him?

  _____

  _____

  _____

DAY 2 – THE BIG PICTURE

He will be great and will be called the Son of the Most High; and the Lord God will give Him the throne of His father David; and He will reign over the house of Jacob forever; and His kingdom will have no end.
(Luke 1:32-33)

I grew up in the late '60s and early '70s. The Spirit of God was blowing through this nation causing what we now know as the Jesus movement. I was a teenager during the Jesus movement. Coffee house ministries were big. Hippies were coming in, getting saved, and becoming *hippies for Jesus.* Calvary Chapel (Chuck Smith) and Vineyard (John Wimber) had their roots in the Jesus Movement. Among musicians who influenced the era were Keith Green and Larry Norman. The wind of revival was riding on a renewed love of worship and the music of the church was changed forever. You may remember those days.

God's desire is to set a wind blowing again in our country even greater than the Jesus movement. Because of His love for the world and desire to be glorified God wants a new worship movement. The movement begins with you today and your personal relationship with Christ. Your job in the process is to set your sail so you can catch the wind of God. You were created to worship something or someone. But for you to be part of a worship movement God must do a new work in your heart. How important is the work? Paul David Tripp explained:

Every human being is a worshiper, in active pursuit of the thing that rules his heart. This worship shapes everything we do and say, who we are, and how we live. This is why the heart is always our target in personal ministry. [1]

God desires to be glorified in who we are and how we live so people can know Him. I see the beginnings of a worship movement, but we must avoid the danger of letting worship experiences, styles, and methods become idols. Every great movement of God produces counterfeit movements. We do not worship great music and emotional worship experiences. We worship the King of Kings and Lord of Lords who transforms our hearts as we worship Him.

God's desire is to wake up the body of Christ and make His name great. I am passionate about these truths. Jesus described His death this way, "And I, if I am lifted up from the earth, will draw all men to Myself" (John 12:32). As we worship Jesus Christ the focus shifts from us to Him and His greatness. When people separated from Jesus see Him as He is, they will be attracted by His beauty.

Why do I have a vision for a movement of God through worship? Because I love music? Of course, I love music. Because I enjoy great worship experiences? Nobody loves those times more than me. But my worship is not about me but about Jesus Christ, the Son of the Living God. I want people to know His greatness: "For it was the *Father's* good pleasure for all the fullness to dwell in Him, and through Him to reconcile all things to Himself, having made peace through the blood of His cross; through Him, *I say*, whether things on earth or things in heaven" (Colossians 1: 19-20). The greatest goals of any believer are to know Him and make Him known.

Our music, energy, and excellence in worship may not be attractive to people who have yet to meet the Lord. But a person authentically worshiping Jesus Christ is a beautiful thing! What is so beautiful about real worship? The beauty of worship is the object of our worship, "One thing I have asked from the LORD, that I shall seek: That I may dwell in the house of the LORD all the days of my life, to behold the beauty of the LORD and to meditate in His temple" (Psalm 27:4). I challenge you to set sail with our beautiful Savior in the days to come.

Debrief with God - *Read John 12*

- What first attracted you to Jesus?

  _____

  _____

  _____

- How has your attraction to Jesus grown over the years?

  _____

  _____

  _____

- In what areas of your life does Jesus rule as king?

  _____

  _____

  _____

- In what areas do you struggle most with His kingship?

  _____

  _____

  _____

- What life adjustments are needed in response to these questions?

  _____

  _____

  _____

- How can you express what God has said in a prayer to Him?

_____

_____

_____

DAY 3 - MY ULTIMATE PRIORITY

The people whom I have formed for Myself, will declare My praise.
(Isaiah 43:21)

You may know what it is like to be forced to live someplace far from where you want to be. Most of us have experienced those feelings whether through leaving home for school or a job transfer. God's people were in a state of extreme homesickness in Isaiah 43. The Babylonians had made them both prisoners and slaves. They were far from home in a place they hated with a people they hated. Their life situation was bad and they were behaving badly as a result.

God comforted His people in spite of themselves. He reassured them that He had all things under control and would ultimately free them from the bondage they hated. He promised better days ahead. He told of something new coming in Isaiah 43:19, "Behold, I will do something new, Now it will spring forth; Will you not be aware of it? I will even make a roadway in the wilderness, Rivers in the desert." Whatever was coming, it had to be an upgrade from what was already there!

We often obsess when God seems to say no to us but we forget to praise Him when we get what we want. God told His people how to respond when He comes through for them. God wants worship to be a DNA issue in our lives or a natural, encoded part of how we relate to Him. He used a striking example to explain: "The beasts of the field will glorify Me, The jackals and the ostriches, Because I have given waters in the wilderness And rivers in the desert, To give drink to My chosen people" (Isaiah 43:20). Not only will the beasts of the fields including jackals and ostriches glorify God but His own people will too! What a shame to think that wild animals will worship God but domesticated man could be too tired or self-absorbed to worship Him!

The thought of growing tired of God or taking His provision for granted seems ridiculous but it happens. Often church and God become such a routine part of our lives that worship becomes merely an external function like going to the post office or grocery store. We have only a *form of godliness* warned against by Paul (2 Timothy 3:5) so we miss His miraculous, powerful intervention in our lives.

The Christ-follower who makes worshiping Jesus Christ his ultimate priority discovers that worship communicates Good News to those who have yet to meet Him. We enjoy a personal relationship with a great God who is actively involved in our lives. Our spiritual journey is not all about us but someone greater than us. Jesus' mission on earth was not to create another religion. The world has had plenty of religions for thousands of years. Jesus is the light of the world. He came to show us the Father, provide a path to get to Him and invite us into a relationship with Him.

God predicted how His people would respond to His great work for them. God saw the future when He said, "The people whom I formed for Myself, will declare My praise" (Isaiah 43:21). The original Hebrew word for *declare* describes how we are to respond to God's activity in our lives. We are to keep meticulous records or lists (like a scribe or secretary) of the great things that God does and tell or sing them out loud.

The word *praise* describes a song to a celebrity or a superstar. So God fully expects us to keep score on His behalf. He is not intimidated by His score being made public. In fact, He loves it! He is blessed when we sing loudly about His greatness so all the world will be drawn to Him. If you really want to find God's people in the future follow the trail of the loudest praise and join in there. Look for the party celebrating the great things that God has done.

The ultimate priority of your life is worship. Jesus was once challenged with a question by religious leaders in Mark 12:28 - *What commandment is the foremost of all?* They probably thought Jesus would reach back into the 10 commandments to give a religious answer, but He didn't. I've worked with religious people since I was a boy. They can be rigid and challenging. Jesus was talking to some hyper-religious people in this passage when He answered: "And you shall love the Lord your God with all your heart, and with all your soul, and with all your mind, and with all your strength" (Mark 12:30). Life with Christ includes making right choices but the relationship is not based on rules alone.

The most important commandment is to love God and worship *is loving God*. Worship places the highest value on the object or person worshipped not the religious act or emotional experience.

How do you act when you're around God? Do you love Him with your whole self? Do tell Him what you think about Him? Do you adore and worship Him? When you love God you will become more like Him. He loves your neighbor, right? So as you love God you will love who He loves. That makes life with Him all fit together and make perfect sense. He gives you a heart to love your neighbor. God described His people as "a people custom-made to praise me" (Isaiah 43:21 MSG). Worship focuses your heart, mind, soul and strength on loving God above everything and thus becomes your ultimate priority.

Debrief with God - *Read Isaiah 43*

- What bad situations do you currently face?

  _____

  _____

  _____

- What promises and reassurances from God can help you?

  _____

  _____

  _____

- What needs to change in your life to make worship your ultimate priority?

  _____

  _____

  _____

- How can you express love to a neighbor this week in a tangible way?

  _____

  _____

  _____

- How can you express what God has said in a prayer to Him?

  _____

  _____

  _____

DAY 4 – GOD IS LOOKING FOR WORSHIPERS

For the eyes of the LORD move to and fro throughout the earth that He may strongly support those whose heart is completely His.
(2 Chronicles 16:9)

John's gospel reports the incident of a Samaritan woman Jesus met at a well. Their conversation evolved to the subject of worship. God looks for those who worship Him. A true worshiper should love that thought!

Jesus built a bridge into the woman's life by asking for some water. She didn't expect a Jewish man to ask a Samaritan woman for anything. After a discussion about living water, he talked to her about the way she was living. She responded: "Sir, I perceive that You are a prophet" (John 4:19). He had just told her about her first five marriages and that now she was living with a man that wasn't her husband. He had never seen or heard of her before. She noticed He was different! But she changed the subject (quickly). She preferred a religious debate instead of a personal conduct dialogue.

We are so much like her. When God begins to make us uncomfortable about ourselves we want to turn the conversation to religious practices or deep theological subjects! She said in John 4:20, "Our fathers worshiped in this mountain, and you people say that in Jerusalem is the place where men ought to worship." She turned the conversation into a religious statement that in no way related to their current conversation. Yet Jesus took the conversation where she wanted and still called her to a new worship life:

Jesus said to her, "Woman, believe Me, an hour is coming when neither in this mountain nor in Jerusalem will you worship the Father. You worship what you do not know; we worship what we know, for salvation is from the Jews. But an hour is coming, and now is, when the true worshipers will worship the Father in spirit and truth; for such people the Father seeks to be His worshipers. God is spirit, and those who worship Him must worship in spirit and truth." (John 4:21-24)

Jesus taught four lessons about worship:

1. *If our lives are wrong, our worship is wrong.* Sin is an obstacle to true worship no matter how religious we might be. God will make us uncomfortable as a consequence. For us to go deeper in worship, we must allow God to go deeper in us. We must let Him make the necessary adjustments in our lives for us to grow in Him and with Him.

2. *Jesus is the focus (salvation is from the Jews) of true worship.* Salvation is not about keeping religious rules or understanding deep theological concepts. Salvation is a relationship with Jesus Christ. The woman explained her belief that a Messiah was coming. I wonder what it felt like to be her at the moment of discovery when Jesus said, "I who speak to you am He" (John 4:26). This encounter with Jesus changed her life forever. Worship would no longer be on her check list of religious duties but would be about her personal relationship with Jesus.

3. *Worship is not confined to a specific place or action.* During your 30-day journey, we hope this will become clearer to you. In public gatherings, you will experience great times of worship. But remember to take what you learn in public into your private life. Jesus said worship is not about places called sacred by religion (John 4:21). The *why* we worship is more important than where we worship. Worship is to be with our lives (serving God) and our lips (praising God). God seeks those who truly worship Him wholeheartedly.

4. *Worship is spirit and truth.* Some people believe worship is all about truth. Jesus said twice that real worship included both *spirit and truth.* Knowing who Christ is and what He has done is knowing truth. Truth is a person – Jesus Christ (John 14:6). But we embrace truth with great humility, because truth without heart is arrogant and divisive. Truth alone often results in dry and dusty legalism (strict rules and regulations). Jesus came to deliver us from the law not to give us strong opinions. My daddy would hold up his Bible to me and say, "Ray, this is a sword, not a club; it is supposed to be a weapon against Satan not a weapon to use in order to beat up our brothers."

We have been guilty of taking the Word of God and beating up each other with it in the name of God. You can take God's Word, twist it around like you want, and pretty much prove anything. Many have done that over the years. In fact, entire cults are built on this flawed misuse of scripture. Yet God's Word is life to those who are looking for Christ, not death.

*For other people w*orship can be a frenzied, emotional experience. Although it may feel good, worship can be like eating cotton candy. There's no real nutritional value, but it feels really nice in your mouth. When we worship with our spirit alone our experience turns into emotionalism. Jesus was saying that both truth and spirit are present in real worship and God looks for those worshipers, "for such people the Father seeks to be His worshipers" (John 4:23).

Jesus informed us about the Holy Spirit: "But when He, the Spirit of truth, comes, He will guide you into all the truth; for He will not speak on His own initiative, but whatever He hears, He will speak; and He will disclose to you what is to come" (John 16:13). Great experiences, exciting singing, quality music, waving hands and even falling on the floor are not necessarily *spirit and truth worship*. When both spirit and truth are part of the worship experience there will always be a sense of love, joy, celebration and sincerity present.

A focus on worship often makes people uncomfortable in the body of Christ. When you add human fears and preferences into a worship conversation, things can get really messy. However, keeping these fears in perspective is critical to the future of a supernatural movement of God. How much do we really control anyway? The ultimate perspective is that we test our worship by Jesus' criteria – spirit and truth.

My biggest concern is for people who are okay with the idea of God, yet are resistant to going deeper with Him. What if He asks you to do something that you do not want to do? What if He shows you something you need to stop doing? Real worship will never keep God at a distance. He will get uncomfortably close (as with the Samaritan woman). He will get in your personal space and begin to rearrange your life. Work past the discomfort, watch, and be amazed at what He will do in your life!

Debrief with God - *Read John 4*

- Which of the four worship lessons was most important for you?

  _____

  _____

  _____

- How will you implement the lesson in your worship life?

  _____

  _____

  _____

- What is God making you feel uncomfortable about in your life?

  _____

  _____

  _____

- What do you need to do next to address the discomfort?

  _____

  _____

  _____

- How can you express what God has said in a prayer to Him?

  _____

  _____

  _____

DAY 5 – MINISTERING TO GOD

And every created thing which is in heaven and on the earth and under the earth and on the sea, and all things in them, I heard saying, "To Him who sits on the throne, and to the Lamb, be blessing and honor and glory and dominion forever and ever."
(Revelation 5:13)

I can remember the night when the Lord blew me away with a new perspective about worship. My worship life was revolutionized as a result! *Worship is to the Lord.* I was listening to a sermon on a November night in 1986. The preacher read Acts 13:2, "While they were ministering to the Lord and fasting, the Holy Spirit said, 'Set apart for Me Barnabas and Saul for the work to which I have called them.'" The early church in Antioch was led by the Holy Spirit to send out the first missionaries in history. The sermon was not about what happened before the sending. Yet that night I noticed that the sending happened: "While they were ministering to the Lord." I did not hear another word after that!

I began in ministry when I was 14 years old, but it was years later when this truth came alive to me. I previously thought worship leadership was my ministry to people for the Lord. Now I realized my ministry was to the Lord with people. From that day, everything changed in my approach to worshiping God.

I cross-referenced other scriptures during the message (and I've apologized to that pastor since). I discovered this passage:

But the Levitical priests, the sons of Zadok, who kept charge of My sanctuary when the sons of Israel went astray from Me, shall come near to Me to minister to Me; and they shall stand before Me to offer Me the fat and the blood, declares the Lord GOD. "They shall enter My sanctuary; they shall come near to My table to minister to Me and keep My charge." (Ezekiel 44:15-16)

There it is again! Worship is my ministry to the Lord. At first I struggled with this idea. Really? Why would God want anything I could give Him? Why would God want my ministry? Does God need something from me? I discovered, in a new way, that I was created in His image. So He does not want just *something* from me, He wants *everything*!

I thought to myself, "Now all I'm really supposed to be doing is ministering to God!" Re-read the Ezekiel passage above and circle every reference God makes to Himself. He sounds like a jealous God, doesn't He? Yet God is the audience when we worship and we are all in the choir. We are priests who minister to Him. Real worship is all about Him, not us! Our question when we approach worship is not, "What can I get from God?" Instead, the right question is, "What can I give to God?"

God's word is clear that we are His priests: "But you are a chosen race, a royal priest-hood, a holy nation, a people for God's own possession so that you may proclaim the excellencies of Him who has called you out of darkness into His marvelous light" (1 Peter 2:9).What do priests do? They deal with all matters concerning worship, and they worship. Priests minister to the Lord.

After the death of Jesus Christ everything changed including the priestly role. His blood was the last blood sacrifice ever needed for us. The veil of the temple was torn from top to bottom exposing the Holy of Holies where only priests previously entered. Now all those who believe have direct access to God as priests.

Under the new covenant, we're asked for a different sacrifice. "Therefore I urge you, brethren, by the mercies of God, to present your bodies a living and holy sacrifice, accept-able to God, which is your spiritual service of worship" (Romans 12:1). We are priests, but instead of a blood sacrifice, we are to present our bodies as a living sacrifice. A blood sacrifice sounds gruesome, but in comparison to the New Testament sacrifice, not so much. The Old Testament required the life of a goat or a lamb. In the New Testament, the sacrifice was a commitment from a person to die to self and live for Christ!

The book of Hebrews gave another major priestly duty. "Through Him then, let us continually offer up a sacrifice of praise to God, that is, the fruit of lips that give thanks to His name" (Hebrews 13:15). We are priests who are appointed by God to offer sacrifices to the Lord! God is asking us for two sacrifices: The sacrificed offering of our *lives* and unashamed offering of praise from our *lips*.

God has given us such authority and responsibility in this life! What an amazing thought! To think that the One who created us and died for us can be blessed by something we do to Him is an awesome revelation. As priests, we give our lives as a living sacrifice. Then, from our lips, there should flow a never ending sacrifice of praise.

Debrief with God – *Read Revelation 4*

- What is the most revolutionary lesson you have learned about worship?

  _____

  _____

  _____

- How did that lesson influence your worship life?

  _____

  _____

  _____

- What part of being a living sacrifice to God is the most uncomfortable to you?

  _____

  _____

  _____

- What step do you need to take to fully embrace being a living sacrifice to God?

  _____

  _____

  _____

- What would it look like for you to offer more praise sacrifices from your lips?

  _____

  _____

  _____

• How can you express what God has said in a prayer to Him?

_____

_____

_____

DAY 6 – FOREVER WORSHIP

Never again will anything be cursed. The Throne of God and of the Lamb is at the center.
His servants will offer God service—worshiping, they'll look on His face, their foreheads
mirroring God. Never again will there be any night. No one will need lamplight or sunlight.
The shining of God, the Master, is all the light anyone needs.
And they will rule with Him age after age after age.
(Revelation 22:3-5 MSG)

Worship is not a fad but an eternal practice. Worshiping on earth is like practicing for heaven. I've talked about heaven a lot over the years. Jokes and stories about seeing loved ones are common parts of every day conversations. We don't have a lot of word pictures of heaven in the Bible so there is some degree of mystery about what heaven will be like. Heaven is really beyond our imagination and like nothing we have ever experienced. What pictures we have in Scripture include sitting around the throne adoring Jesus, the One who got us there!

John, in the book of Revelation, described the most sensational worship experience in history. The time, date, and place are yet to be determined. Notice the focus was not the method of worship or even the worship leaders. The band, sound and style are incidental. Worship is focused on the most worthy Lamb of God! He is the focus of our worship now, too. How much relational tension in churches would be bypassed if the Lamb became the single focus! My friend, Dennis Jernigan, wrote a worship song that captures this sensational worship experience in Revelation.

We Will Worship

We will worship the Lamb of glory
We will worship the King of kings
We will worship the Lamb of glory
We will worship the King

And with our hands lifted high, we will worship and sing
And with our hands lifted high, we come before You rejoicing
With our hands lifted high to the sky
When the world wonders why
We'll just tell them we're loving our King...Oh
We'll just tell them we're loving our King.
-Dennis Jernigan [1]

Read through all of Revelation 4-5 if you want to enjoy a great personal worship time. John described the worship this way:

> And when the living creatures give glory and honor and thanks to Him who sits on the throne, to Him who lives forever and ever, the twenty-four elders will fall down before Him who sits on the throne, and will worship Him who lives forever and ever, and will cast their crowns before the throne, saying, Worthy are You, our Lord and our God, to receive glory and honor and power; for You created all things, and because of Your will they existed, and were created. (Rev. 4:9-11)

> And every created thing which is in heaven and on the earth and under the earth and on the sea, and all things in them, I heard saying, To Him who sits on the throne, and to the Lamb, be blessing and honor and glory and dominion forever and ever. And the four living creatures kept saying, "Amen." And the elders fell down and worshiped. (Revelation 5:13-14)

What a picture! Can you imagine the scene in heaven? Worship is the natural response to someone we adore. We cheapen worship when we try to guilt or manipulate people into being excited about Jesus Christ. Worship is so much greater than manufactured experiences. Worship is discovering who Jesus really is face to face. Authentic excitement follows that great discovery. God longs for us to worship Him unashamed, unhindered and unforced. When we are truly with Him (Revelation 4-5), we get to that incredible place.

Christian musician and worship leader, the late Keith Green, once asked the question, "Will we be bored in Heaven?" In his article he made a powerful and convicting observation:

> The Lord made me realize recently that if I do not absolutely relish His company now, desiring to be with Him more than anyone in the whole world, then I would not really be comfortable in heaven at all - for it is there that we will spend all eternity in the company of the Holy One who made us.[2]

If you don't like worship here, you'll be miserable in Heaven! You will be bored stiff! We will adore the One who loved us first for eternity. Revisit these great passages that reveal who Jesus is. Reconsider where you are in your relationship with Him. He will ignite a new flame of passion for Him when you do.

Debrief with God – *Read Revelation 5*

- What picture of Heaven made the greatest impression on you?

_____

_____

_____

- How can this picture help you take your personal worship to another level?

_____

_____

_____

- What is the greatest obstacle to your passion for worship?

_____

_____

_____

- How can you address this obstacle and reignite your worship life?

_____

_____

_____

- How can you express what God has said in a prayer to Him?

_____

_____

_____

DAY 7 - THE WORSHIP CYCLE

But you are a chosen race, A royal priesthood, A holy nation, A people for God's own possession, so that you may proclaim the excellencies of Him who has called you out of darkness into His marvelous light.
(1 Peter. 2:9)

I (Dino) will never forget the day a lady sat in my office in New Orleans and asked a question God wanted me to hear. She was trying to decide whether I was fit to be her pastor. She said, "Jesus said, you should love the Lord your God with all your heart, soul, and mind."

Then she asked, "Do you?"

She made it harder by refusing to accept anything but a *yes* or *no* answer. That day I realized I didn't take His command personal enough. And if I was not obeying the first one, none of the others really mattered. Following Jesus is actively loving and serving the King of Kings. Living by religious rules and regulations says nothing about my love for Christ.

Worship is loving God. Jesus gave a famous answer to an important question. A lawyer asked which of the commandments was the greatest. Jesus answered, "You shall love the Lord your God with all your heart, and with all your soul, and with all your mind" (Matt. 22:37). The key word in the passage is **all**. Loving God with *all* of you (heart, soul, and mind) is a lifelong journey with Jesus Christ.

The first step to genuine worship is the realization that God is bigger than you. We are created to worship and all of us worship something or someone. If we choose to worship God, it requires the outpouring of our deepest affection and is crowned with our personal sacrifice. Worship is a choice.

Isaiah was a sad and anxious prophet before his meeting with God (Isaiah 6). He seemed to be living by the rules of God but was distracted by the drama of everyday life. Can you relate? I can. Living by the rules was not enough. He needed to love God on a deeper level.

A major crisis drew Isaiah to deeper places with God. His friend King Uzziah died. The political and personal implications were staggering. Isaiah had lost a friend and his friend had made terrible choices before he died. God's people were now more vulnerable to a hostile takeover by Assyria's evil ruler who was determined to be king of the world. What happened in Isaiah's dramatic meeting with God?

God met with Isaiah during the most difficult days of Isaiah's life. When Isaiah experienced God's presence he was changed forever. He fully surrendered to God's mission at a time when most leaders would have run away. When God moves, He gives his people courage. Isaiah learned who really was King. Neither Uzziah nor the evil king from the north were actually in charge. God was seen seated on a throne as King of the world.

Much of life is connected to a cycle. Winter, spring, summer, and fall happen each year. When one ends the other begins. You often hear history repeats itself. Worship is no different with five basic elements that make up a cycle. When we live within the parameters of a worship cycle an unending process keeps us in constant communion with God.

When I plan worship, I go through these elements so that there will be continuity for worshipers. When I attend a worship gathering I remind myself of these elements to enhance my experience with God. The elements are: praise, adoration, confession, listening, and obedience. When we are obedient to God's voice it will lead us back to praise. This cycle will continue as long as we desire an intimate relationship with God.

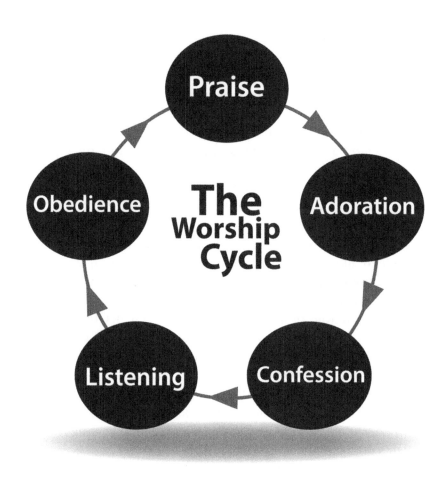

I have taught "The Worship Cycle" for many years now. In a recent worship experience, I was reminded of the cycle again. God was certainly present in the *praise* and celebrative phase and we all knew the sweetness of His presence during the *adoration* phase. When we got to the *confession* phase God led me to share a deep need in my life. This was the *listening* phase. Although hesitant, I obeyed – which completed the cycle (the *obedience* phase).

God spoke to the needs of other people through my experience. We opened the altar for others that had needs that day. The altar was filled at the front, on the sides and even halfway up the aisles. God spoke; the people listened and then obeyed. God's intervention led us to a season of celebration and praise for what He had done. After the service I realized how The Worship Cycle had happened before my eyes.

I am convinced that every believer is somewhere in The Worship Cycle every day! After we first did *Will You Worship?* at Community Bible Church, I had one lady tell me how liberating this teaching was to her. She was more aware of personal worship and the presence of God in her life on a daily basis. She said, "Now I know each day where I am in the cycle." She got it!

Like Isaiah we all deal with deep personal pain and disappointment that influences our life with Him. Each day this week read Isaiah 6. Keep notes in this journal about what God shows you. Also practice a greater awareness of where you are in the cycle. Watch God continue to transform you as a result!

Debrief with God – *Read Isaiah 6*

- What makes these days difficult for you?

  _____

  _____

  _____

- What do you need from God most now?

  _____

  _____

  _____

- Where are you in *The Worship Cycle*?

  _____

  _____

  _____

- What or who can keep you moving?

  _____

  _____

  _____

- Who can you encourage this week that is facing difficulties now?

  _____

  _____

  _____

• How can you express what God has said in a prayer to Him?

_____

_____

_____

DAY 8 – CELEBRATING GOD'S GREATNESS

At that very time He rejoiced greatly in the Holy Spirit, and said, I praise You,
O Father, Lord of heaven and earth, that You have hidden these things from the wise and
intelligent and have revealed them to infants. Yes, Father, for this way
was well-pleasing in Your sight.
(Luke 10:21)

During my first years at Community Bible Church there was a contingency of people who wanted us to be more conservative in our approach to worship. Nevertheless, my heart was to be intentional and consistent in our approach to help our people experience the presence of the Lord. We were convinced that when we accomplished this, eternal things would happen in their lives. We prayed for years that a spirit of celebration would take place every week in our services. Now God has given us a culture of celebration where our people enter each week with great expectancy.

Early in our tenure at this church, we realized that we were going to be a *doorway* church. So many new believers were coming in that introducing spiritual concepts to our congregation would be an ongoing process. When we relocated in 1999 to our present property, we had carpet in the front part of our worship center and a gym in the back.

We often referred to the people who understood our worship concepts as the carpet people. Our goal was to get people in the doors and see them mature into the carpet people, who were fully engaging in worship. One of my current worship staff members was one of the gym worshipers who moved to the carpet, and then to the microphone -- that was a fun process to watch.

Isaiah was invited into a worship encounter with the King of Kings in Isaiah 6. His world was filled with anxiety. His trusted friend, King Uzziah, had recently died a miserable failure. The terrible King of Assyria, backed by the power of his great armies, aspired to rule the world. But soon Isaiah could walk in freedom because of his vision of the King of Kings! Isaiah's perspective was revolutionized by this encounter with God. The vision of God's glory would provide encouragement for the difficult days ahead.

Praise. *The first element of The Worship Cycle is praise.* Praise is celebrating God's greatness. We find an example of this in Isaiah 6. Isaiah saw a dramatic vision of God and was made aware that there was greatness in the room through the praise. Seraphim (angels) surrounded the presence of God with praise drawing Isaiah's attention from himself to an incredible God:

> *Holy, Holy, Holy, is the LORD of hosts,*
> *The whole earth is full of His glory.*
> (Isaiah 6:3)

Praise declares to God and others what we know about who He is. When we praise Him we answer the question, "Who is God?" The angels answered God is *Holy, Holy, Holy*. In this instance the angels pointed out His perfection, purity and superiority over all armies who might overtake Him as King of the world! Worthy of praise! All the attention in the room belongs to Him! Praise is the doorway into the presence of God and it begins a wonderful cycle of worship. He is holy, powerful, and greater than all others.

The Bible frequently shows God's people as a people of praise:

- *The LORD is my strength and song, And He has become my salvation; This is my God, and I will **praise** Him; My father's God, and I will extol Him* (Exodus 15:2).

- *It is good to give thanks to the LORD, and to sing praises to Thy name, O Most High* (Psalm 92:1).

- *Enter His gates with thanksgiving, and His courts with praise. Give thanks to Him; bless His name* (Psalm 100:4).

There is such joy in our worship at Community Bible Church that it may seem irreverent at times. In reality, I don't see our movement into the presence of Jesus as being anything but celebrative because of His greatness. He is superior in every respect and full of excellence.

Another picture of praise is seen in Matthew's version (21:1-11) of Jesus' entry into Jerusalem. We see a gift of the passionate Jewish culture – celebration! His chosen people really knew how to celebrate. People were often greeted this way as they entered the city, particularly people of importance. You have to wonder what was noteworthy about the son of a Jewish carpenter, riding a lowly donkey. But remember, praise is *recognizing the superiority of Jesus over all others*. Praise answered the question, "Who is Jesus?" Jesus is the King of Kings, and is worthy of our loudest and most active celebrations.

Anxiety is high in our current culture. Many of us come from fractured families and have made our own share of mistakes. We face an uncertain economy and have never felt more vulnerable as a nation since 9/11. Culture offers us entertainment in abundance from Netflix, to the internet, to our personalized iPods. We have learned to numb our disappointments through entertainment that often becomes addictions. In the midst of all of this we have lost our ability to celebrate. We are bored and depressed. Praise for who God is will give us a revolutionary new perspective! Worship shifts our attention from culture and personal pain to the King of Kings!

Praise, indeed is the doorway into the presence of God. Praise and thanksgiving are exciting, majestic, unashamed, celebrative and often loud. Praise brings believers into God's presence and announces to the lost and hurting that the King is in the room!

Debrief with God – *Read Matthew 21*

- What habits or hobbies are distracting you from the presence of God?

  _____

  _____

  _____

- What can you change to spend more time in the presence of God?

  _____

  _____

  _____

- What part of your past is disturbing you the most today?

  _____

  _____

  _____

- How can God help you revisit your past to give it a proper burial?

  _____

  _____

  _____

- What is your next step?

  _____

  _____

  _____

- How can you express what God has said in a prayer to Him?

  _____

  _____

  _____

DAY 9-LOVING GOD LAVISHLY

Yours, O LORD, is the greatness and the power and the glory and the victory and the majesty, indeed everything that is in the heavens and the earth; Yours is the dominion, O LORD, and You exalt Yourself as head over all.
(1 Chronicles 29:11)

A sense of awe and wonder captures us when we are in God's presence. Adoration is our first response. We are reminded in Isaiah's story of God's awesome presence: "And the foundations of the thresholds trembled at the voice of him who called out, while the temple was filling with smoke" (Isaiah 6:4). Have you ever met someone famous who you idolized and adored? Personally, I stumble over what I say and fear saying something that may be offensive.

Adoration is the second element of The Worship Cycle. Adoration is loving God lavishly. As dangerous as it sounds, at the point of my greatest adoration is my greatest vulnerability. I can be shaped by the will of the One I adore! Isaiah, the voice to his generation, was in such awe and fear that he was utterly speechless. He witnessed the angels hovering around the King of Kings with their faces covered to honor Him. Isaiah entered the greatest palace he had ever seen to meet the greatest King in history and eternity. After the initial shock had passed, he began to show his deep adoration for his God. He was brought to the place where he could soon respond to the Father's question, "Who will go?" He was shaped by the will of the God he adored.

Praise is how we get into God's presence, but adoration is what happens when we arrive. Adoration answers the question, "How will I honor Jesus?" In today's culture we would describe adoration as *going over the top* in honor and admiration. Adoration gives honor or weight to Jesus Christ.

We see examples of adoration throughout Scripture. In Luke's Gospel, we see an example of an immoral woman who adored Jesus:

And there was a woman in the city who was a sinner; and when she learned that He was reclining at the table in the Pharisee's house, she brought an alabaster vial of perfume, and standing behind Him at His feet, weeping, she began to wet His feet with her tears, and kept wiping them with the hair of her head, and kissing His feet and anointing them with the perfume. (Luke 7:37-38)

This woman had experienced the life-changing message of Jesus' forgiveness and acceptance. Why else would she adore Him so extravagantly? What a contrast to Simon, the hyper-religious Pharisee, who invited Jesus into his home to attempt to entrap Him. Her culture was zealous in showing honor to others. The common Middle Eastern custom of washing the guest of honor's feet was ignored. The absence of such a greeting was not simply an oversight but an intentional insult.[1] When we gather weekly in our worship venues, it is incredible to think that the most honored guest often goes unnoticed. Often times we put in our best efforts to welcome *prospective* members. Yet we ignore the King of Kings who stands outside at the door and knocks.

What is the reality in the story? The Pharisees (Simon in particular) felt alienated from Jesus because His message was so foreign to their belief system. The sinful woman felt fully loved and completely forgiven by Him. The result was her unbridled adoration. Completely forgiven people adore Jesus Christ. Adoration is a heart issue.

The purpose of the *Will You Worship?* Project is not to train you to become a worshiper. We pray that God will do a work in your heart that will, in turn, begin to influence the depth of your worship life. As you surrender, you place yourself fully in the hands of Jesus to be transformed into His image. This project simply focuses your worship on the God who transforms you into a worshiper.

The immoral woman in the story boldly entered into a room where she was unwelcome to do something for Jesus that the religious Pharisees refused to do. She did not care what the Pharisees thought of her. She had no personal accomplishments that would possibly impress Jesus. She was another grateful recipient of His grace. Out of her brokenness she wept as she knelt at the feet of her Savior. Her wet tears fell on His dry, dusty feet. Showering her Redeemer with affection, she began to kiss his road weary feet.

Religion and culture could have caused Jesus to refuse her adoration. Yet Christ was above religion and culture. She took her hair, the Jewish woman's crown of glory, and wiped the dirt and tears off His feet. Finally, she took a bottle of costly, scented ointment and graciously massaged his feet as an act of service and love. This is the picture of genuine adoration. Focused on a person not on a religious practice, the woman exalted the guest of honor in the room. She was intentional in her expression. She was a worshiper.

Debrief with God - *Read Luke 7*

- When or where do you sense the presence of God the most?

  _____

  _____

  _____

- What are ways you can respond the next time that happens?

  _____

  _____

  _____

- What areas of your life have been touched most by the grace of God?

  _____

  _____

  _____

- How can you show greater affection and admiration to Jesus Christ?

  _____

  _____

  _____

- How can you express what God has said in a prayer to Him?

  _____

  _____

  _____

DAY 10 – ADJUSTING MY LIFE TO GOD

Therefore, if anyone cleanses himself from these things, he will be a vessel for honor, sanctified, useful to the Master, prepared for every good work.
(2 Timothy 2:21)

I was sitting in a hotel room in 1988 listening to a television evangelist make a public confession of his sin that shocked the nation. At that point, God spoke to my heart and said, "In the last days I am going to use faceless men and women." Celebrities will come and go. But God most often uses ordinary people in extraordinary ways for His glory. Broken people who have been put back together by Him are the most useful in His hands.

I once had a set of golf clubs that I could never hit very well with, so a friend suggested that I get the grips replaced. I followed his advice with great results. My game improved dramatically in spite of the fact that they were the same clubs. What was useless became useful in my hands. The process of brokenness involves God taking the same personality, talents and giftedness and simply refitting them to His hands. Why? So He can use them in a more effective manner.

Brokenness is the first step to personal transformation and is part of adjusting my life to God. God invites us to worship Him and begins to transform us when we accept His invitation. Brokenness is experienced when we stop comparing ourselves to others and start comparing ourselves with God and His holiness.

Isaiah was so buried in bad circumstances he could have lost his vision of God. Everyone in his life had disappointed him and he had perfectly good reasons to be terrified about the future. He could have easily fallen prey to a victim's mentality but his encounter with God changed all that. What a lesson for us to learn! We are often a chronically angry and frustrated people. We are angry at the world and the church for being sinful. Bad circumstances, however, are no excuse for missing God's mission.

In real worship God shows us His holiness. His holiness puts a spotlight on our un-holiness. Then, the sins of others become less significant. We realize how sinful we are and that changes everything. Our mission becomes a mission of grace. After Isaiah's encounter in God's presence God's mission came into focus. Isaiah received a clearer picture of God's grace and His plan to send the Wonderful Counselor (Isaiah 7:14).

Broken things are no longer useful. The only hope for something broken is to be fixed by someone greater! When we find ourselves in the presence of God we begin to see ourselves in the light of His holiness. We see ourselves full of darkness and as part of the problem. Then we confess our sins saying: "Woe is me, for I am ruined! Because I am a man of unclean lips, And I live among a people of unclean lips; For my eyes have seen the King, the LORD of hosts" (Isaiah 6:5).

Confession. At the point of our greatest uselessness becomes our greatest potential! *The third element of The Worship Cycle is confession.* Confession is adjusting my life to God. Confession that I am part (or all) of the problem is a big step for most of us. Confession means that I come into total agreement with God about my sin and take ownership of my part of the problem. When we enter the presence of God in worship, brokenness and confession will soon follow.

Confession is agreeing with God that I have sinned and adjusting my life to His holiness. When I confess I answer the key question, "What disappoints God about me?" When I see sin as God sees sin, it is not a pretty picture. This experience does not stop at confession. Confession brings awareness of sin yet more is needed. Repentance is the critical next phase. That means I was going my own way with great confidence. Yet at a point in time I was arrested (busted) in my sin. I realized that my way was not God's way. Then, I made a u-turn back to His way. The very essence of our Christian faith is when God arrests us in our sin and we make a u-turn to go back (to Him).

The benefit of repentance is the presence of God, according to Peter's sermon in the book of Acts: "Therefore repent and return, so that your sins may be wiped away, in order that times of refreshing may come from the presence of the Lord" (Acts 3:19). True repentance leads you back into the presence of God.

A few years ago a lady came to me who was broken about her sin. After confessing where she had been and what she had done her question was, "Can God use someone like me?" I said to her, "You are the only kind of person God can use." God uses broken things. Some may say that you are disqualified by your sin but God says, "I will forgive you and because you are repentant I will use you."

Broken people are trophies of God's grace and billboards announcing sinners can be made valuable through the power of God. Now she stands week after week singing the song of the broken and restored to all that will listen. God will use you after He breaks you. Then He gets all the credit for your new life.

Debrief with God - *Read Psalm 51*

- What place of personal darkness (sin) are you hiding from God and others right now?

  _____

  _____

  _____

- What steps do you need to take to bring the darkness to the light of Jesus?

  _____

  _____

  _____

- How can you invite others into the healing process?

  _____

  _____

  _____

- How can you help someone who has recently experienced failure this week?

  _____

  _____

  _____

- How can you express what God has said in a prayer to Him?

  _____

  _____

  _____

DAY 11 – EMBRACING GOD'S HEART

My sheep hear My voice, and I know them, and they follow Me.
(John 10:27)

One Sunday morning as I was walking into church a little boy ran up to me, grabbed my leg and said, "Remember, it's God's Day!" I stopped in my tracks. I was reminded that God was the reason for our gathering and had no doubt He had something to say. Hearing God is a vital part of any worship encounter.

God spoke to me in an unusual way when I was leading worship at a deacon's retreat in Alabama. While leading a song I sensed God telling me to stop and share the gospel. I had plenty of excuses for God not to do this. I thought, *God, these are deacons in their churches and they are all already saved. I am not the speaker today and the leaders might be offended.* God was not impressed with my excuses and opinions about what was best.

So, I stopped leading worship and shared the gospel with the group. From the back of the room a 78-year-old man walked forward and prayed to receive Christ. He then stood before all those deacons and told them how he had never committed his life to Christ. He had been ashamed to admit his lack of relationship with Christ because he was a leader in the church. God had the last and best word. He saw what I could not see.

God always speaks at the appropriate moment and what He says may not always make sense to us. Often we miss what He says because we insist the message make sense or it must not be Him. Many times, as is the case at this deacon's retreat, the opposite is true.

God only speaks to those whose hearts are prepared to hear and obey. Proclamation is the element of worship when God speaks. Up to that point He was simply enjoying hearing from His kids. He loves to hear His children worship.

Isaiah's story was full of drama. Do you know what has not happened yet in the story? God has yet to speak. A powerful worship experience is never an end to itself. God will ask us to do something and attempt to move us. He finally breaks silence to ask in Isaiah 6:8, "Whom shall I send, and who will go for Us?"

Listening. *The fourth element of The Worship Cycle is listening.* Listening is embracing God's heart for the world. The most important question ever asked by anyone is, *What does God want?* In this instance God wanted someone to go for Him. He is a God who seeks lost people. When we listen to Him we will embrace His heart and seek lost people.

God speaks more often than we hear Him but most of the time we are too busy talking. The Worship Cycle describes the daily life of a Christ-follower beyond the Sunday morning experience. Enjoying His presence, hearing His voice, and obeying His orders describe daily life with God.

When God spoke in Isaiah's story He only said a few words, "Whom shall I send, and who will go for Us?" (Isaiah 6:8). God may speak through a sermon, a testimony or a song. However, He is not limited to any of these. God also speaks through circumstances, people and Scripture. He can speak to you during your daily routine. Obey His promptings.

Often someone will tell me after a worship service that God spoke to them about something specific. At times what God said to them was not specifically mentioned in the sermon or in a song. God's sermons and songs are what He uses to open hearts to His voice. His message often goes beyond the particular agenda for the day. When you are experiencing The Worship Cycle, God can speak at any time and use anyone or anything to communicate His will to you. Your job is to always be ready to listen and obey.

Debrief with God - *Read John 8*

- What did God say the last time you heard Him speak to you?

  _____

  _____

  _____

- What do you need to do to continue obeying Him?

  _____

  _____

  _____

- What environments does He use to speak most to you?

  _____

  _____

  _____

- What can you do this week to create those environments?

  _____

  _____

  _____

- How can you invest time and prayer this week in someone who has yet to meet Christ?

  _____

  _____

  _____

• How can you express what God has said in a prayer to Him?

_____

_____

_____

DAY 12 – FINDING MY PLACE

*I glorified You on the earth,
having accomplished the work
which You have given Me to do.*
(John 17:4)

When you experience The Worship Cycle and God speaks clearly to you, what is your next step? Isaiah's answer was to give his life to God's plan when he said, "Here am I. Send me!" Authentic worship prepares the heart to say *yes* to Him. That is one great test to your worship life. Saying *yes* is the first step of obedience. Do you know what the second step is? Following through and doing what Jesus asks.

Notice that Isaiah said *yes* to a pretty vague request. He got answers only after he said *yes*. The same is true in your life. Those things that are obstacles to obedience now may be answered in time. But why should God answer questions when the answers matter only after you obey? Some other responses from Isaiah would have been perfectly understandable:

- *Where am I going?*
- *When do I leave?*
- *Can I take people with me?*
- *Who will take care of my needs?*
- *What am I supposed to do?*
- *How long will I need to stay?*
- *Who will help me?*

Obedience. *The fifth element of The Worship Cycle is obedience.* Obedience is finding my place in God's plan. God was looking for a *yes* man (or woman). Isaiah's worship experience left him totally surrendered to whatever God wanted. He became God's blank check. When God gives you a question, you should always answer it immediately. Delayed obedience is the same as total disobedience. When the God of the universe takes time to speak, we should take it seriously.

I came from a traditional church background where we often had *invitations* or *altar calls* for people to walk to the front of the auditorium at the end of the sermons. The pastor would announce the number of *decisions* made by the people who responded. But everyone in the room responded to God's message, not just the people who walked forward. They may say, "Yes." Or, "I'm not sure." Or, "No, I am not going to obey you, Jesus." Every one of you will respond to what God is saying to you right now. Notice that...

Noah said *yes* to God when everyone else said *no*.
David said *yes* to God and Saul said *no*.
Isaiah said *yes* to God and Jonah said *no*.
John said *yes* to God and Judas said *no*.

In all cases everyone responded. Because God loves you, He invites you someplace with Him and for Him. What about you? What is God saying to you? How will you respond?

We know God is speaking, that is not the question. The question is, "How will you respond?" If your answer is, *"Yes, Lord,"* it leads you back to praise, thanksgiving, adoration, brokenness, listening and obedience. Can you see the pattern? God's activity in the life of one who loves Him always includes movement to someplace new. Our responsibility is to find our place in His plan.

Are we there yet? We are making progress but have more places to go. We want you to grow deeper in your personal worship life with Jesus. You have been at it for two weeks and God's picture should be coming into focus. Worship is a place we go with God where He lovingly confronts and changes us. No one stays the same in His presence. Real worship is so much more than great music and good feelings. Real worship is standing in God's presence completely surrendered to Him.

Debrief with God - *Read John 17*

- What area in your life do you need more answers from God?

  _____

  _____

  _____

- What questions do you need to surrender to God?

  _____

  _____

  _____

- What answers could you discover now through further prayer and research?

  _____

  _____

  _____

- What is one big thing you learned on your worship journey so far?

  _____

  _____

  _____

- How has that changed your worship?

  _____

  _____

  _____

• How can you express what God has said in a prayer to Him?

_____

_____

_____

DAY 13- ACTIVE WORSHIP

O clap your hands, all peoples;
Shout to God with the voice of joy.
(Psalm 47:1)

Remember the television sales commercials that would never end at the first offer? The announcer would say, "But wait! There's more!" God has so much more to offer in life than most people ever experience. He has solutions that we could never discover or dream up on our own. God's Word delivers the, "But wait! There's more!" message from cover to cover. The difference is God is not selling anything. He gives all things for free! Read these affirmations of God's goodness:

- *How great is Your goodness, which You have stored up for those who fear You, which You have wrought for those who take refuge in You, Before the sons of men!* (Psalm 31:19).

- *Therefore the LORD longs to be gracious to you, And therefore He waits on high to have compassion on you for the LORD is a God of justice; How blessed are all those who long for Him* (Isaiah 30:18).

- *But just as it is written, 'Things which eye has not seen and ear has not heard, and which have not entered the heart of man, all that God has prepared for those who love Him'* (1 Corinthians 2:9).

Today we come to a turning point on our worship journey. The first two weeks we have focused on heart issues. We examined the stories of the woman Jesus met at a well and the discouraged prophet/preacher Isaiah to learn how deep God really wants to go in us. Worship is an issue of the heart, right? When Jesus gets all of us He will change everything about us.

The turning point is moving to the activity of worship. We started at the right place – the heart, but now we will look at the actions of a worshiper. The goal is to paint a picture of a person who actively loves God through worship. Then put yourself in the picture! What an incredible thought! What if 100 or even 1000 people in a local church entered the picture at the same time? Jesus Christ would be put on display and communities would be turned upside down for Jesus Christ as a result.

What does it really look like to worship? I am talking about a "real time" example of people actively engaging the God of the universe with love and admiration. Picture a person who has made worship a priority and who has identified where they are with God. Now they are free to let the activity of worship begin. Psalm 100 is filled with worship action words. Every worship encounter does not need to look like Psalm 100. The Bible is full of pictures showing different worship encounters. But Psalm 100 is a great example to consider.

I never had little girls in my home – my children were all boys. You know what having sons looks like in your home if you have ever been to a three-ring circus. My home had plenty of action, in plenty of places, with never a dull moment. My sons would fly, scream, dive, and fall.

The room is so different when my sweet and beautiful granddaughters are there. Little girls are active in their own way. They sit on the floor while they talk, giggle, and play. Boys are active in their own way. Although we all do not necessarily need to worship like little boys and girls play, authentic worship will involve a variety of active responses. Who we are and what God says influences those responses.

Psalm 100 invites us to come into God's place and tell Him He is great! Notice in the Psalms we are constantly being invited to go someplace with God. What a high compliment to us, as well as a description of God's grace. God wants us in His presence. He is not annoyed or put off with us and we really don't get on His nerves. He does not look down at the planet Earth and say, "Wow, what a great place if it were not for the people." He invites us into His holy presence by asking, "Will you worship me?" or, "Will you go somewhere with me?"

My dad challenged me to memorize Psalm 100 when I was a boy. Through the years I have used it hundreds of times while leading worship. Over the rest of the week you will discover seven action statements that teach how to go someplace with God to worship.

Debrief with God - *Read Psalm 33*

- What is your biggest obstacle to growing deeper with God in worship?

  _____

  _____

  _____

- Who can you talk to that might help you work through the obstacle?

  _____

  _____

  _____

- What would a deeper worship life look like for you one year from now?

  _____

  _____

  _____

- What would you need to change for that to happen?

  _____

  _____

  _____

- How can you express what God has said in a prayer to Him?

  _____

  _____

  _____

DAY 14 – MAKE NOISE

With trumpets and the sound of the horn
Shout joyfully before the King, the LORD.
(Psalm 98:6)

A lifelong dream came true for me in 2010. I was raised in Louisiana and spent a great deal of my ministry in New Orleans. My favorite football team, the New Orleans Saints, won the Super Bowl for the first time in history. You may not be a sports fan or a Saints fan, but the Super Bowl was particularly big for New Orleans. They had been trying to win a Super Bowl since 1966. For all those years they were known as one of the biggest sports losers in history. Fans even wore bags over their heads to games because they were so embarrassed about how bad the Saints were. I saw it firsthand.

When they won the 2010 Super Bowl, I shouted. In fact, I shouted so loud that I think the whole neighborhood heard me and I didn't care. I was traveling the day after the Saints big win, and I saw some other New Orleans Saints fans in the airport. We all started shouting again. The Saints deserved my shout and I gladly gave one up for them. I had fun! I was unashamed and uninhibited when it came to giving a victory cheer for my Saints!

We use our voices to communicate both the positive and negative. Our voices express our deepest passions and our most important concerns. My dog, Cooper Jack Jones, once broke into our storeroom and pulled the kitty's bed out into the yard (among other things). I gave Cooper Jack a lot of my passion that day. I confess I shouted my feelings about the situation. My dog heard my voice and he immediately got the message. With great remorse he seemed to repent of his evil deeds toward our kitty and me. His deepest desire was to be my friend again. My point here is that my shout showed my passion about the situation, and it got a positive response.

We live noisy lives. Most of us are relieved that making noise is not a requirement in order to know and worship God. A familiar Psalm even gives us permission to be quiet as a part of our active worship: "Be still, and know that I am God. I will be exalted among the nations, I will be exalted in the earth" (Psalm 46:10 ESV). At times God chooses to speak and move in quietness. He is God; He can speak anytime and anyway He chooses. But to engage God fully in worship *making a joyful noise* with our voices is a vital next step.

Worship is loving God. I don't want to make worship more complicated than necessary. Yet a refusal to engage God on a more passionate level with our voices could be a heart issue disguised as a preference. You may say *that's just not me* as your reason for passionless, voiceless worship. Make sure your lack of passion is not a stubborn, prideful heart issue.

Psalm 100 describes a passionate expression of worship demonstrated through our voices: *Make a joyful noise to the Lord. Noise* is used in the original Hebrew language to describe using one's voice as an alarm or a war cry. Our voices are described as instruments of worship we use for God just like a guitar, piano, or violin. You never raise your voice unless you are passionate about something. This verse gives permission and a command (whichever you need) to be passionate about God, and let Him know it with your voice.

Notice Psalm 100:1 does not say shout *about* the Lord but shout *to* Him. We use the term *vertical worship* to describe an important principle that will help you grow as a worshiper. In the past, our worship gatherings have mainly focused on singing about the Lord. Some precious and meaningful songs have been written that way. However, the next level is singing and shouting to the Lord or vertical worship.

Vertical worship is our faces looking upward to Him and our songs being presented to Him. He is the audience when we worship and we make our presentations to Him. Remember in the first week of *WYW,* I told the story about my revolutionary discovery: *worship is our ministry to the Lord.* We see the principle of scripture repeated again in Psalm 100:1 as we do throughout the Psalms. The next level in our worship is engaging God directly when we worship. Praise is His and He loves to hear it. Such shouting comes from a heart full of joy.

Why does God seldom move us as deeply as a football team or a mischievous dog? God deserves our loudest cheer and our deepest passion. A victorious war cry given to God is in order! Not only is God winning but God wins! Give your best noise to God with joy and abandonment. Go beyond the token or obligatory offering of praise and singing. Be bold in your expression so that God will know of your passion for Him. One thing I can promise you, God will never grow weary or impatient with you for being too excited about Him.

Debrief with God - *Read Psalm 98*

- What is most awkward to you about shouting to the Lord?

_____

_____

_____

- What are some ways you can make your worship more vertical (God-focused)?

_____

_____

_____

- What part of worship are you the most passionate about?

_____

_____

_____

- What part of your heart does God need to capture for you to engage Him more deeply?

_____

_____

_____

- How can you show the love of Christ in a practical way to a neighbor this week?

_____

_____

_____

• How can you express what God has said in a prayer to Him?

_____

_____

_____

DAY 15 – SERVE AND SING

Therefore I urge you, brethren, by the mercies of God,
to present your bodies a living and holy sacrifice,
acceptable to God, which is your spiritual service of worship.
(Romans 12:1)

During our study of *The Purpose Driven Life* by Rick Warren at Community Bible Church, we made a new discovery. Worship is more than what happens in the first 30 minutes of the weekend services. Not only is our worship an act of service to the Lord but our service is an act of worship.[1] The Bible used the words worship and service interchangeably. For our service to be effective it must be with a happy heart because when you serve you offer a gift of worship to God. You also show the world how important God is when you serve Him.

What did the psalmist mean in Psalm 100:2 when he challenged us to serve the Lord with gladness? The word *serve* was commonly used to describe the work of a slave. Although slavery was common in Bible history, that did not make it a good thing. But if you were going to be a slave, the God you loved and worshiped would make a great master. He truly loves and cares for you. Your relationship with God has other implications. Not only am I looking at a tough assignment (slavery), made great by my real master (God), I now have the opportunity to be glad (extreme pleasure and delight) as I serve. What a different approach to life!

Psalm 100 is in reference to serving in the temple, but it is applicable to any service to God. Working with children, or in the nursery rocking a baby to sleep, greeting people or directing parking lot traffic can all be worship when done for God. Like with Brother Lawrence (*Practicing the Presence of God*) it is all a matter of attitude. Do you see God there? Do you serve for Him? Then your action can be worship.

Worship is a vertical relationship with God. That means I am 100% focused on Him. Anything I consciously do for Him is worship. Worship is everything I do if I am conscious that everything I do is for God and with God. If we are going to worship God 24/7 then we must embrace this idea. Yes, you can worship God out on the lake if what you are doing is for Him and with Him.

Worship can be everything we do but the idea concerns me if not properly applied. However, the perspective can revolutionize our lives if we get it. If we say worship is everything we do then we risk making worship too common and almost accidental. And my greatest fear is that if worship is everything then worship becomes meaningless.

Worship is loving God, so perspective is everything. If everything you do is intentionally given to God and shaped by your love for Him, then worship is everything you do. The implications of such an attitude are far reaching and the positive influence for Jesus can be great. What would you stop doing if you were convinced that everything you did was worship? What would you start doing better?

My pastor's dad, Mr. Harry Emmitt, was a successful salesman for a major pharmaceutical company. He traveled extensively, but every weekend he was home and stationed outside his church as a greeter. He greeted people each morning with a loud and happy, *Well, Good Morning*. Everyone knew Mr. Harry and he was loved by all. He was not a teacher, he did not sing and he wasn't a pastor giving sermons. He was just Harry Emmitt giving his service of worship to his King. He understood the concept, *Serve the Lord with gladness*.

Worshipers are also invited in Psalm 100:2 to, "Come before Him with joyful singing." Have you noticed how often we use singing to express our feelings about important times, places and people in our lives? We sing at birthdays, holidays, and vacations. Did you also notice none of us really care if the singing is not all that great?

Singing is a fun way to celebrate and connect with our friends. We sing at ballgames, school events, weddings, and graduation ceremonies. Singing is a universal way of showing you care about someone or something. Singing shows unity toward a cause and it evokes the emotion of the singer and the listener.

I am amazed our attitude about singing at church contradicts how we feel about music in daily life. "I just can't sing," people say, "I am just not any good at it or no one wants to hear me sing." All three statements above might be the truth! However, let me give you this test. Next time you are at your grandchild's birthday party will you use the same excuse when the whole room sings *Happy Birthday*? I don't think you will. You love your grandchild with all your heart. You are thrilled to be with them and want to please them. You will sing from your heart, bad voice and all.

Did you join in singing *God Bless America* at the baseball game when everyone stood during the seventh inning? Were you worried about how you sounded at the stroke of midnight on New Year's Eve? Did you have a hard time singing the fight song for your alma mater during the homecoming game? I think you are starting to get the point. How about a new focus this week? Sing publicly and privately to the Lord. He loves to hear you, bad voice and all!

Debrief with God – *Read Romans 12*

- How can you take serving God through your local church to the next level?

  _____

  _____

  _____

- If *everything* you did this week was a worship gift to God what would you stop doing?

  _____

  _____

  _____

- If *everything* you did this week was a worship gift to God what would you do better?

  _____

  _____

  _____

- What would make singing to the Lord easier for you in public and private?

  _____

  _____

  _____

- How can you engage in your favorite worship music on a daily basis?

  _____

  _____

  _____

• How can you express what God has said in a prayer to Him?

_____

_____

_____

DAY 16 - GET TO KNOW GOD

That I may know Him and the power of His resurrection and the
fellowship of His sufferings, being conformed to His death.
(Philippians 3:10)

Worshipers are Christ-followers and Christ-followers are worshipers. You can't separate one from the other. Passion to follow and love Jesus is to recognize who He is – He is Lord (boss). How else would you respond to your Lord but to worship Him? So if to follow Jesus is to be a worshiper of Jesus then the next statement will make more sense: The single greatest reason there is no passion for worship is that people have yet to meet Jesus personally.

We *welcome* anybody at Community Bible Church in San Antonio. We leave plenty of space for people to process their spiritual journeys. Yet for the *insiders* who have met the Lord, worship means something more than attending church. To know Jesus is to worship Him.

So I invite you to know Jesus. Psalm 100 specifically identifies a God who is worth knowing. God is not anything you decide you want Him to be. I respect the space people need for a spiritual journey and understand that some move faster than others. But my heart is that you would be heading in the right direction on your journey. My heart is that you would discover the God of the universe through a relationship with His son, Jesus Christ. The psalmist issued an invitation: "Know that the LORD Himself is God; It is He who has made us, and not we ourselves; We are His people and the sheep of His pasture" (Psalm 100:3).

Three big ideas in Psalm 100:3 will help you move forward in your journey:

- *He is the only God, the Lord, He is God* – Your spiritual journey is with Him alone.
- *He created us* – We did not accidently evolve or appear after a big bang.
- *We belong to Him* – He wants to reclaim us as His lost children.

I hope this helps you feel valued and loved. Since all the above is true, don't you think He is a God worth knowing personally? How do you get to know God? The more time we spend in someone's presence the more we know them. Think about your wife or family. Is there anyone who knows you better than they do? Why? The days, the months, and the years that you have spent with each other have caused you to know each other well.

Worship is the place where we get to know God intimately. Have you ever been alone and started singing as if your only audience was God? You should try it; you will like it. The practice of being in His presence is how we mature in our knowledge of God.

As you read this journal I feel compelled to stop you and ask, *Do you know Jesus?* Knowing the facts about Jesus or admiring Him is not enough.

Do you have a personal relationship with Christ?

The Bible teaches that we can know Him as a person through a relationship. The Bible tells us how to begin that relationship. A dear friend and mentor, Leo Humphrey, would explain it this way: "There are two things to know and one thing to do…"

First you must *know* that you are a sinner and that you need forgiveness for your sin. Romans 3:23 says, "For all have sinned and fall short of the glory of God." That means ALL. You and I have this in common with everyone in the world. We are natural-born sinners who tend to choose for ourselves and against God.

Second you need to *know* that your sin will separate you from God for eternity. Romans 6:23 tells us, "The wages of sin is death but the free gift of God is eternal life." Sin is costly yet you have the opportunity to choose where you spend eternity. Best of all, if you choose Heaven it is a free gift to you paid for by the death of our Lord Jesus on the cross.

Finally, the one thing that you must do is found in **Romans 10:9-10**, "That if you confess with your mouth Jesus as Lord, and believe in your heart that God raised Him from the dead, you will be saved; for with the heart a person believes, resulting in righteousness, and with the mouth he confesses, resulting in salvation."

Now, this involves belief and surrender. The belief is that Jesus is the Son of God who died on a cross and rose from the grave. Then, confess that *Jesus is Lord* or your boss for eternity. God is so eager for you to follow Him that He made the plan simple. If you believe and surrender to Jesus Christ, He will save you. The greatest decision I have ever made was years ago when I crossed the line to faith in Jesus Christ through belief and surrender.

If you want to know Him I suggest you stop right now and pray this prayer of belief and surrender below. Nothing is magic about the prayer. Nothing happens inside you unless you are seriously committed to following Jesus:

Lord Jesus, I know I am a sinner and need forgiveness from my sins. I invite you into my life and ask you to forgive me. I give you my life and ask that you make me the person you want me to be. Thank you for loving me. Thank you for dying on the cross for me. I love you Jesus, Amen.

Debrief with God - *Read Philippians 3*

- What is your next step in your relationship with God?

  _____

  _____

  _____

- Who do you need to talk to about that step?

  _____

  _____

  _____

- What would it take for you to spend more time alone with God in the next week?

  _____

  _____

  _____

- What would make the time alone most valuable?

  _____

  _____

  _____

- How can you express what God has said in a prayer to Him?

  _____

  _____

  _____

DAY 17 – ENTER WITH THANKS AND PRAISE

Be anxious for nothing, but in everything by prayer
*and supplication with **thanksgiving***
let your requests be made known to God.
(Philippians 4:6)

We played football often in our backyard when I was a boy. One day a few boys were involved in a big game at my house. We threw the ball over my neighbor's fence several times during the game and I would simply jump the fence to get the ball. At one point during the retrieving process things turned bad. I jumped the fence, caught my shoe on the top of the chain link, and planted my face into the wire mesh on the other side. My pride and body was severely damaged. My face looked like I had lost a fight with a waffle iron.

As I tried to recover, I decided to go around and use the gate to get back to the game. As I passed by, my Dad gave me some great advice. He said, "Son, next time use the gate." His advice is still good for the growing worshipers. Use the gate God provides to enter His presence. Many seem to peer into His presence from the outside yet never enter in. He provided clear access to His presence by the way of thanksgiving and praise. Real worship can be foreign to us and overwhelming. Where do I start? The answer is in the gates and courts of Psalm 100.

Thanksgiving and praise are critical worship starting points. Thanksgiving is telling God how we feel about what He has done for us. Praise is telling God what we think about His character. Remember that:

- *Thanksgiving is personal* because we talk about what God did for us.
- *Praise is global* because it speaks of God's impact on everyone in the world because of His nature.

Worship includes acknowledging personal and global realities about God. The God of the universe is great and this great God loves me. He owns the cattle on a thousand hills (*global*- Psalm 50:10) and takes care the ravens (*personal* – Luke 12:24).

Psalm 100 teaches we are to *enter His gates with thanksgiving*. Are we ever guilty of getting what we want from God to make our lives better and ignoring Him after that? At times I am guilty. William Barkley once said, "So often, once a man gets what he wants he never comes back.[1]" The God of the universe has done so much for us. We all deeply desire to be close to Him and sense His presence. We could be one *thank you* away from being closer to God.

Worship is a love gift to God. You would never think of giving God a bad gift, right? If God came to visit your home would give Him leftovers or a beat up gift from your garage? Would you stand, arms folded and coldly greet Him as He entered your home? When we give God our thanksgiving and praise we give Him our best. We would welcome and bless Him lavishly.

When I do something for one of my four sons and they respond with genuine gratefulness something inside of me wants to do more. In my experience with my Heavenly Father I see that is His nature as well. We should never show gratitude to the Father with an ulterior motive, but God loves a grateful heart and He rewards those that are thankful.

What reasons do we have to say *thank you* to God? Here is a great exercise. Picture yourself living out in the middle of a vacant lot. You are cold, sick, hungry, and in physical pain. You have a dirty, tattered shirt, a pair of pants that are too small, and no shoes. No family, no job, no money, no friends, no relationship with God is there to help. Nobody knows or cares about you. You are an invisible *zero* in every sense of the word. Now write down, starting at zero, everything and every relationship you have in real life, one thing at a time. You have more than you thought don't you? As God shows you His blessings say *thank you* for each one.

My pastor, Robert Emmitt and I, have been working side by side for over 19 years. We have a good working relationship and I know he respects me as a co-laborer. Occasionally, after a Sunday worship gathering, he will text me a gracious thank you note. The note not only encourages me but motivates me to do even more to provide great worship experiences for our congregation.

Gratitude moves people to work harder and accomplish more with a joyful attitude. So it is with God; His blessing rests on those that have grateful hearts. When Israel showed God gratitude with their offerings God always reciprocated with His abundant blessings.

As a leader when I give praise to my co-laborers for their character it always amazes me how they respond with humility but it also super charges their Kingdom efforts. When pure thanksgiving and praise to God goes out . . . He responds by supercharging the atmosphere of our worship. The psalmist said, "Yet You are holy, O You who are enthroned upon the praises of Israel" (Psalm 22:3). You can experience the presence of God when your life is filled with praise and thanksgiving. You can dwell in His courtyard by continually praising Him.

Debrief with God - *Read Luke 17*

- What are some material blessings from God that you may have overlooked?

  _____

  _____

  _____

- Who are some people God has used to bless you that you may have overlooked?

  _____

  _____

  _____

- How can you say thank you to them in a way they would notice?

  _____

  _____

  _____

- How can you build better patterns of thanks and praise to God?

  _____

  _____

  _____

- How can you model a life of thanks and praise to God to help those around you?

  _____

  _____

  _____

- How can you express what God has said in a prayer to Him?

  _____

  _____

  _____

DAY 18 – SAY GOOD THINGS

Bless the LORD, O my soul,
And all that is within me, bless His holy name.
Bless the LORD, O my soul, and forget none of His benefits...
(Psalm 103:1-2)

The concept of blessing God may be new to you, particularly when you are giving the blessing. Most of us were taught that God will bless us, but we never heard that we should bless God. Blessing God is one of the most freeing and gratifying principles of faith. For years I would receive a blessing and then pass it on to others, operating as a conduit for God. That falls short of God's full intent. He desires for us to bless His name.

Our tongue is an instrument of honor to God when we speak blessings to Him. The Bible teaches us of the awesome potential to do damage with our tongues. I have seen this principle played out in the lives of thousands of prison inmates. Many of these prisoners were told from an early age that they were bad and would never do anything right. Sadly, that curse was fulfilled in their lives. The same tongue, however, has the potential to worship and talk about God. The tongue that blesses can influence people in a powerful way and when it blesses the name of the Lord the floodgates of Heaven open.

The tongue can either be our best friend or our worst enemy. A powerful description of the tongue is given in the Bible, "But no one can tame the tongue; it is a restless evil and full of deadly poison. With it we bless our Lord and Father, and with it we curse men, who have been made in the likeness of God; from the same mouth come both blessing and cursing. My brethren, these things ought not to be this way" (James 3:8-10).

Our choice of either blessings or curses is simple. To *bless* means to *compliment, speak well of, to praise, salute, or greet*. We get our English word *eulogy* from the Greek word. But don't save your compliments for funerals. Your loved ones would enjoy hearing them while they are still alive. Say good things to God about God! Say good things to people about God. You will go deeper with Him and for Him when you do! And when people overhear your compliments to God they will want to get to know Him too!

I have coached boys' basketball for 20 years and I have learned that my tongue can change the momentum of a game. We were playing for the city championship several years ago and my team came out intimidated by their opponents. Nervous and afraid, they made all kinds of mistakes. So to add to their fear I called time out and verbally beat them up. I said things like, "You are better than this. Don't you remember anything we have practiced? You guys are not giving me maximum effort." They walked out of that time out totally defeated and did even worse than before.

At halftime, we trailed by 18 points. If we continued to play scared we would have no chance to make it a game. Before the second half began I called the boys in and said, I want you guys to know that I believe in you and that you are a blessing to my life. We have had a great season and have 16 minutes left to win or lose. I want you to do two things, play defense well and go have fun."

Although we did not win the game we closed the lead to six points and played like champions. With the simple choice of using my tongue to bless and not curse, the environment around me was changed.

A hymn I sang numerous times in church growing up really speaks to the excitement that should fill our hearts in active worship. The hymn, *O for a Thousand Tongues* was written in the early 1700s by a man named Charles Wesley. Wesley was celebrating 11 years of being a Christian when a friend inspired him by a comment. His friend said to him, "Oh, Brother Wesley, the Lord has done so much for my life. Had I a thousand tongues, I would praise Christ Jesus with every one of them!" What a powerful tool God has given us in our tongues. If only we had 1000 tongues, we could bless Him with each one! Wesley wrote:

O for a thousand tongues to sing
My dear Redeemer's praise,
The glories of my God and King,
The triumphs of His grace![1]

Debrief with God - *Read James 3*

• How can you bless God more this week?

_____

_____

_____

• Who can you tell a good word about God to this week?

_____

_____

_____

• Who can you build up this week with blessing?

_____

_____

_____

• What negative (curse) talking needs to change in your life?

_____

_____

_____

• Who could you ask to pray for you and keep you accountable?

_____

_____

_____

• How can you express what God has said in a prayer to Him?

_____

_____

_____

DAY 19– READY FOR DINNER?

God, who gets invited to dinner at your place?
How do we get on your guest list?
(Psalm 15:1 MSG)

So far we have taken three steps into a deeper place of personal worship. First, we discovered God invites us to worship Him. Jesus met a woman at a well and their discussion turned to what real worship was about. He told her God was looking for real worshipers. Second, we discovered that God's purpose in worship is to transform us. He never intended worship to be merely a great experience. He invites us to worship Him and when we go, we are changed. Isaiah was a great example of what God does in a person who enters His presence. Then, God sends us to our friends, communities, and nations to make Him famous. We become living invitations to a relationship with God.

God is a missionary God. We can't possibly be close to Him as a worshiper without being sent somewhere for Him. The sending process begins with the *invitation* to worship. However, the critical phase of sending is *transformation*. God invites, God transforms and God sends. Imagine a movement of hundreds and even thousands of people who accept God's invitation to worship Him in a way they never have before. What would God do? How would He transform those people? What difference would they make for Him when sent back into their world?

Remember we set out to define worship in the simplest terms possible. We are complex people so the best place to start with God is simple. What is worship? ***Worship is loving God***. Let's break this down.

First, worship is extraordinary. We say, "I worship the ground she walks on," to describe strong feelings about someone we love -- but we are being a bit dramatic. Could you imagine coming upon your teenage son on his knees, in his sock feet, sobbing loudly, with his hands raised? You lunge toward him scared that some terrible thing has happened to him. You wrap your arms around him and say, "Son, what's the matter? Did someone hurt you? Were you robbed? Are you sick?"

He answers, "No daddy, see this spot right beneath me? My girlfriend walked right here, yesterday morning, in this very place. She is the most beautiful girl on the planet. Take off your shoes and bow with me! You are standing on holy ground!"

Our time, energy and money are given to important things and people every day of our lives (and unimportant things, too). Yet worship is a unique action in a unique relationship. Worship is reserved for God alone as the most extraordinary and valuable relationship above all. My relationship with God is like none other! Jeremiah the prophet said it this way:

There is none like You, O LORD; You are great, and great is Your name in might. Who would not fear You, O King of the nations? Indeed it is Your due! For among all the wise men of the nations, And in all their kingdoms, There is none like You. (Jeremiah 10:6-7)

When we place the highest value on our relationship with God, we grow into a greater awareness of that relationship. Thus, worship *is* in the present tense. We may have great memories of worship experiences in our past but we can't live off yesterday. Our greatest times of worship are times when *His presence is present*. We walk away from those times not only encouraged, but changed. Yet the real experience of His presence is like manna in the wilderness. The greatest value of the manna of God's presence is that it is here all the time. Our consciousness of His presence in real time is a key to loving Him.

Brother Lawrence spent 18 of his early years in the French Army. He was never considered successful. Later in life, at the urging of his uncle, he became a lay brother in a Paris monastery. For 30 years he worked in the kitchen and shoe repair shop until his death. A short collection of his letters and stories called, *The Practice of the Presence of God*, is a Christian classic. He had an unusual sense of God's presence in his every day life. Brother Lawrence said:

We can do little things for God; I turn the cake that is frying on the pan for love of him, and that done, if there is nothing else to call me, I prostrate myself in worship before him, who has given me grace to work; afterwards I rise happier than a king. It is enough for me to pick up but a straw from the ground for the love of God.[1]

God's people in the Old Testament were tempted to worship other gods and were often guilty. God constantly reminded them of His position in the universe. The most famous reminder is known in Jewish history as the *Shema* which means *to hear*:

Hear, O Israel! The LORD is our God, the LORD is one! You shall love the LORD your God with all your heart and with all your soul and with all your might. These words, which I am commanding you today, shall be on your heart. You shall teach them diligently to your sons and shall talk of them when you sit in your house and when you walk by the way and when you lie down and when you rise up. You shall bind them as a sign on your hand and they shall be as frontals on your forehead. You shall write them on the doorposts of your house and on your gates. (Deuteronomy 6:4-9)

Did you see it? God gave us a picture of what it would look like to practice and live in His presence.

Here is the expanded version of what we are trying to communicate:

Worship   [the highest and most unique action in my life]
is   [every conscious moment, every day]
loving   [expressing fondness through acts, attitudes, and acknowledgment]
God   [the one and only God of the universe]

No question, as with Brother Lawrence, simple directions have big ramifications for how we approach God daily. The key word(s) are practice, practice, practice!

Debrief with God - *Read Jeremiah 10*

- What is distracting you from your relationship with God?

  _____

  _____

  _____

- How can you address that distraction?

  _____

  _____

  _____

- How can you practice a greater awareness of His presence?

  _____

  _____

  _____

- Where do you think God is sending you this week?

  _____

  _____

  _____

- How can you express what God has said in a prayer to Him?

  _____

  _____

  _____

DAY 20 - GET READY TO MEET GOD

I was glad when they said to me,
"Let us go to the house of the LORD."
(Psalm 122:1)

I (Dino) am old enough to remember taking a bath in an old wash tub on Saturday night in Tennessee. My grandmother used to heat the water on top of the stove right before bath time. The hot steam would rush to the ceiling as she poured pots of boiling water in the galvanized tub. The tub was just big enough for a little preschool boy to enjoy. Why the Saturday night bath? We were getting ready for the big day! Sunday morning at Little Doe Freewill Baptist Church! I loved Sundays as a child. They were important days. Getting ready for such an important day was critical to making Sundays special in our lives.

God told Moses that His people needed to get ready for a meeting with Him. How interesting! "The LORD also said to Moses, 'Go to the people and consecrate them today and tomorrow, and let them wash their garments; and let them be ready for the third day, for on the third day the LORD will come down on Mount Sinai in the sight of all the people'" (Exodus 19:10-11). God wanted His people to never view meeting with Him as common or unimportant. Meeting with Him should not be one thing to do on a checklist with many other things in a day. The original form of the word *consecrate* is where we get the word *holy* or *belonging to God*.

A preparation process before meeting with God is essential. Even if it is in an old wash tub! Setting aside time to pray, focus and prepare to meet God will make a difference in how well the meeting goes. A focus on the externals can remind us that our hearts need to be prepared too. Visualize the galvanized wash tub in Tennessee or the fresh washed garments at the base of Mount Sinai. The call to experience God's presence is the call to prepare!

Psalm 15 was an invitation to worship God that considers another aspect of worship preparation. In fact, this is as important as the *wash tub prep* the night before. David challenged worshipers to prepare by the way they lived their lives before the worship moment. We will spend the rest of the week talking about this. Worshipers asked questions in Psalm 15:1 like, "O Lord, who may abide in Your tent? Who may dwell on Your holy hill?" They asked the right questions! And the worship leaders gave some pretty tough answers in Psalm 15:2-3 with a list of behaviors and attitudes critical to a life of integrity before God.

We have experienced the undeserved, unconditional love of God in our lives. So, is it awkward to lay expectations at the feet of worshipers? Well, God had expectations throughout Scripture for those who approached Him. God invites us to deeper, transformational places with Him that are worthy of our best efforts and greatest focus. The presence of God is well worth anticipation and preparation.

An old song we sang for years describes our genuine desire to be in God's presence. Joseph Hart described himself as *a monstrous sinner* until Christ rescued him. He wrote these words of personal testimony in 1759:

> *Come, ye sinners, poor and needy,*
> *Weak and wounded, sick and sore;*
> *Jesus ready stands to save you,*
> *Full of pity, love and power.*
> *I will arise and go to Jesus,*
> *He will embrace me in His arms;*
> *In the arms of my dear Savior,*
> *O there are ten thousand charms*[1]

Come ye sinners poor and needy . . . that's us, right? Yet in spite of the fact that we are all sinners we can't excuse our behavior. Over the years I have heard people say things like, *God understands me* to excuse ungodly decisions or habits. Yes, God understands you more than you understand yourself. But His plan for you involves changing who you are.

I heard someone say, "God loves you just the way you are, He just doesn't want you to stay that way." So does God accept your steps toward Him through the eyes of grace and the blood of His Son, Jesus? Absolutely. Yet He has bigger plans for you. If you want to find a deeper and better life with Him you have a responsibility to prepare.

Debrief with God – *Read Exodus 19*

- How can you better prepare for daily worship this week?

_____

_____

_____

- How can you better prepare for your weekly worship gathering?

_____

_____

_____

- What attitude or behavior needs to change for your worship life to grow deeper?

_____

_____

_____

- What is the biggest lesson you have learned over the first 20 days of *Will You Worship*?

_____

_____

_____

- How has your approach to worship changed over your last 20 meetings with God?

_____

_____

_____

• How can you express what God has said in a prayer to Him?

_____

_____

_____

DAY 21 – WHO WILL WORSHIP?

Behold, bless the LORD, all servants of the LORD, Who serve by night in the house of the LORD! Lift up your hands to the sanctuary And bless the LORD.
(Psalm 134:1-2)

Can you relate to this adventure? You get up early Sunday morning to start the coffee and read the newspaper. You sit down alone in the quiet to read the sports page. Sure enough your team won so all is right with the world and God is on His throne. In a few minutes your family begins to stir and you help get breakfast ready.

After everyone is fed they all go to their rooms to get dressed for Sunday morning worship. The activity picks up as the kids start to ask the usual questions: *Have you seen my shoes? Where did you put my socks?*

As the time to leave approaches you notice the pitch in your voice changes as you announce that we need to be gone in 15 minutes. Now the activity is at a frantic pace and the kids begin to act as if they are oblivious to the situation. Finally, you stand at the door, tap your foot, point at your watch and say loudly, *We need to leave right now!*

One by one the group files out the door. You set the alarm and rush to the car. Suddenly the security alarm goes off and you ask the question, *Did anyone put the dog out?* Running back into the house you have to search for the dog because he is scared out of his mind by the shrill sound of the alarm. You answer the phone call and give the alarm password. You reset the alarm and sprint to the car only to find that a WWF wrestling match has broken out in the back seat. Mom is now yelling for the kids to settle down. You get in the car as you swat little legs with your right hand and buckle your seat belt with your left.

As you back out of the driveway you glance back over your shoulder only to see that your youngest child has on one green sock and one orange sock. You begin a discourse on matching colors. Then you look at your oldest, see a large chocolate milk stain on the front of his dress shirt, and you lose it. You yell, *Did you not see that milk stain in the mirror when you were brushing your teeth?* His reply is predictable, *but I did not brush my teeth.* Being a mature man of God you scream, *Everyone shut up, be still and don't touch anything or anyone. WE ARE GOING TO THE HOUSE OF THE LORD TO WORSHIP GOD!!!*

Everyone is now quiet as you get to the parking lot of the church. Because you are late you park in the back lot about a half-mile from the building. You park the car and reach down to get your Bible only to realize that you picked up the mystery novel you had been reading the night before instead. You are now beyond the point of return when out of the morning silence you hear a friendly greeter making his way to your car, saying with a loud voice, *Gooood morning to you, how are you this fine day?* To which you grit your teeth and squeeze out a quiet, *Fine and you?*

Christ-followers often divide life into neat compartments. We have our lives at church activities in one category. The expectations are pretty clear about how people are supposed to act at church so we comply. We have big smiles and say cheerful hellos. Our family is close by our side. We sit next to them during the sermon and talk to them in a nice tone of voice. Songs are sung with gusto. We might even mutter an *Amen* when the pastor says something we like.

Our public selves are never exactly who we are in private. We know how bad it is to be labeled hypocrites or play actors. Yet our public displays, even the *niceness*, are likely who we really want to be. We are just not real consistent at being the people we really want to be. So in public we practice for a better way of behaving for God privately.

Psalm 15 gives us ways to prepare to enter into God's presence on a daily basis. If we were really in God's presence we would behave differently. We would become the people that God wants us to be as well as the people we really want to be. And remember, He *graces* us with His presence beyond what we can ever deserve. Yet Psalm 15 begins and ends with what we really want in life: the daily presence of God that will help us live and stand strong in Him!

How important is worship in the life of God's people? Is worship for the emotional people? Women and children only? Musicians and singers? Pastors? Worship is so important that one day a week was set aside by God for His people to worship in community. So if worship is important then preparing to worship is as important.

Psalm 15 is a song that was written to explain a life preparation process for worship. Do we approach worship under the guise of being perfect people, who just lived a perfect day or had a great week? *Of course not.* But we do approach worship with a willingness and commitment to be as prepared on the inside as we are on the outside.

Have you ever made a checklist before your vacation trip? A great time has been anticipated for months. In the final days and hours preparation is the key to success. Consider worship in the same way. If you are going to make a great connection with God in daily or weekly worship, use Psalm 15 as your checklist. Invest time preparing your heart.

We will unpack the big ideas of Psalm 15 in the rest of this week. But notice the list begins with the basics. I prepare for worship by the way I behave in everyday life (walk). I prepare in relationship with friends and neighbors, as well as the way I handle my resources. You see an overarching value: *As I live, work, and play I will behave in a way that God is glorified and honored.* This is my relationship with Him and thus, it influences the way I worship. ***The Message*** condenses the actions to a simple list:

o *Walk straight*
o *Act right*

o *Tell the truth*
o *Don't hurt your friend*
o *Don't blame your neighbor*
o *Despise the despicable*
o *Keep your word even when it costs you*
o *Make an honest living*
o *Never take a bribe* (Psalm 15:2-5 MSG).

Who will worship? That question is determined by us not God. The condition of the heart determines how we live, and how we live will determine the depth of our worship.

Debrief with God – *Read Psalm 15*

- What area in your life do you feel like you are the biggest hypocrite?

- What step can you take with God to help you grow in that area?

- How can you help your family better prepare for Sunday worship gatherings?

- When can you brainstorm ideas with your family about worship preparation ideas?

- How can you express what God has said in a prayer to Him?

DAY 22 – WORSHIP CHECKPOINTS 1-2

I will lift up my eyes to the mountains; From where shall my help come?
My help comes from the LORD, Who made heaven and earth.
(Psalm 121:1-2)

Over the next three days we will consider Psalm 15 as worship preparation checkpoints. These five checkpoints are values lived out daily. So, preparation for worship is a lifestyle not a point in time event. For most of us they will require an ongoing adjustment of our attitudes and behaviors. Without the power of God these adjustments are impossible. Today we will look at the first two checkpoints.

Checkpoint #1: **Integrity.** *The first preparation checkpoint is personal integrity* (Psalm 15:2). Your personal integrity will determine the depth of your worship. The root of the Hebrew word for "integrity" is being *whole* as opposed to being fragmented. A person without integrity is constantly trying to hide different parts of his life from God and other people.

Being honest with God and others is the pathway to wholeness and integrity. Yet many people live desperate, secret lives terrified of the consequences of being caught. Have you ever wondered why the people with the deepest sin issues in their past seem to be the most free in Christ? Coming out of the closet (in some cases literally) is the way to enjoy freedom in Christ. They have been freed by Christ from fear of rejection and incarceration! They have fully experienced the truth, "So if the Son makes you free, you will be free indeed" (John 8:36).

Their honesty allows them to fully experience the grace and mercy of God. Our secrets keep us from His grace! Think about it.

Confession is agreeing with what God already knows about you and is a great first step to prepare for His presence. The Greek word for "confession" means "to agree with, say the same as." Tell Him the truth about your heart's condition and your failures. Express your deepest fears and greatest needs. This will show Him your desire for His presence. God wants people with pure hearts to worship him.

Matthew said, "Therefore if you are presenting your offering at the altar, and there remember that your brother has something against you, leave your offering there before the altar and go; first be reconciled to your brother, and then come and present your offering" (Matthew 5:23-24).

I see this in a different light as I think about worship preparation. Matthew is painting a picture of a worshiper who failed to prepare. Are you being honest with God and other people? If you are not then you are not fully connecting with God in personal or public worship.

Your prep time with Him puts you on a clear path to a blessed worship experience. But notice that failure to prepare is not an excuse. If you realize that you left something undone you must stop your worship and take care of the unfinished business. Integrity demands you do so. God demands you do so!

God does not play games with you. Listen for His promptings during a worship time and do what He says even if it requires you to stop. Then you will experience a new place of worship for Him. At times in my past, before I could walk on stage to lead worship, I had to make a phone call or seek someone out to apologize for being short or insensitive. What has God been saying to you lately as you worship? How have you responded? Integrity will bring you to a new level of freedom in your personal and corporate worship.

Checkpoint #2: **Consideration.** The second preparation checkpoint is consideration. God desires considerate (healthy) relationships with our friends and neighbors. Are you constantly experiencing relational drama in your life? Did you ever stop and think about the consistent thread in the drama? You are the consistent thread. If every dramatic relationship is someone else's fault in your life it is likely that someone is you! Messy, dysfunctional and impure relationships have a direct impact on your worship life. You may not be able to fix them all before Sunday, but to approach them with more consideration is a great place to start.

How we view people is a direct reflection of where we are with God. Do you love people? Do you accept people who are not like you? God consistently challenges us in His word to relate to others well because our relationships are a reflection of who He is to the world! That's a big responsibility. God gave the world permission to decide if we are real or not based on our love for each other (John 13:34-35). I hope that thought is as heavy to you as it is to me.

My pastor, Robert Emmitt, has talked several times to our congregation about 3 kinds of people: ***uppers, downers and non-effectors***. The *upper* is the person who walks into the room and as a result everyone starts to feel better about their lives. His smile and encouraging words, along with a refusal to engage in negative conversations, is life to the people around him.

The *downer* is the person who walks into the room and as a result the joy leaves. It is as if he sucked the positive energy right out of the place. When you ask him how he is doing he says things like: "I'm making it. Things have been better. I'm doing the best I can."

The *non-effector is* the quiet, unassuming person who really does not want attention. He has no impact on the people in the room. For me it is easy to love the *upper* because he makes me feel better. I have no problem with the *non-effector* because he is low maintenance and requires little energy. But the *downer* is hard for me to love. I want to run the opposite direction when I see him coming.

The application here makes the verse challenging but clear. I am responsible to love the people around me no matter how they impact the room. God gives us no other option than to love and consider others. To do anything else is sinful and has a negative influence on our worship.

Debrief with God - *Read Matthew 5*

• What area of your life are you trying to hide from God and other people?

_____

_____

_____

• How can you address that area in a way you never have before?

_____

_____

_____

• What relationships in your life are causing the most drama now?

_____

_____

_____

• How can you address those relationships in a more positive way this week?

_____

_____

_____

• How can you express what God has said in a prayer to Him?

_____

_____

_____

DAY 23 – WORSHIP CHECKPOINT 3

How blessed is everyone who fears the LORD,
Who walks in His ways.
(Psalm 128:1)

Checkpoint #3: **The Fear and Awe of God.** The third checkpoint is based on the value of being in awe of God (Psalm 15:4). A person *who honors those that fear the Lord* is ready to worship. A healthy fear of God is essential to truly worship Him. When we fear God we naturally *honor those who fear the Lord* too.

The consideration of friends and neighbors in the last checkpoint was directed toward loving those in our world no matter if they love God or not. Yet some do better at their relationships with friends and neighbors than they do with their co-worshipers! The contradiction is that our co-worshipers normally have the same values we do. Shouldn't those relationships be easier? Most relationship drama emerges from conflicting values. Right?

But the devil is alive and well. If he can only prove to the world we are hypocrites (as he tried to do with Job) his hard work pays off for eternity. Remember Satan knows the Bible better than most of us! He knows these verses: "A new commandment I give to you, that you love one another, even as I have loved you, that you also love one another. By this all men will know that you are My disciples, if you have love for one another" (John 13:34-35). One way Satan proves to the world we are hypocrites is by tempting us do something remarkable – hate our co-worshipers!

In Exodus 3:2-6, Moses was tending the flocks when God appeared to him in a burning bush. God captured Moses' attention and instructed him to take off his shoes because he stood on holy ground. Moses was afraid and hid his face from God. He realized how awesome God really was.

Worship is an uncommon event in life. As with God's explanation in Exodus 20, the Sabbath was set aside for us to stop everything, gather together and put all our focus on Him. God must be your life, not just one of many important things in your life.

Oswald Chambers is most famous for writing the devotional classic that has helped millions of people, *My Utmost for His Highest*. He described the priority of our lives with God in a book less famous*:* "It must be God first, God second, and God third, until the life is faced steadily with God and no one else is of any account."[1]

This third checkpoint reminds us to be in awe of God. The Bible says we can be friends with God. Moses was a case in point. But we must not reduce God to our *buddy* or our *super friend*. Our view of God will influence our passion for worship and if we are in awe of God we will experience awesome worship. Reverence is equated with respect and awe. To revere God is to honor Him with your profound respect.

When my wife Andrea was a pilot for US Airways, we took a trip to New York City. We got a hotel room in Manhattan. Andrea and Benjamin took off to go to a Broadway show. Christopher was an infant so I put him in a stroller and we went out to see the city. One place I wanted to see was the famous Times Square Church where David Wilkerson was the Pastor.

At 4:30 p.m., I walked past the front doors of Times Square Church only to see greeters dressed in suits welcoming people into the building. Since it was Tuesday afternoon I asked what was happening. A greeter said with excitement, "Our pastor has called a special prayer meeting for 6:00 p.m. and we are getting ready."

I asked if I would be allowed to go into the building and look around. I explained that I was a pastor from Texas and had always heard good things about their church. He welcomed me in but told me that the prayer team was in the worship center preparing for the prayer service.

I took Christopher out of the stroller and put him on my shoulder. I sat quietly in the middle section at the back. To my surprise there were about 150 prayer warriors at the altar praying. They spread out over the room praying over every seat. As they passed me they laid their hands on my shoulder and on my son. Then they prayed God's blessing on my life and my family.

At 5:00 p.m. they opened the doors and people rushed into the room. A pastor walked on stage and announced that the room was filled and the overflow room was available. On Tuesday at 5:45 p.m. the entire place was packed to capacity for a prayer meeting! When 6:00 p.m. arrived, the stage curtain opened with a full choir and band. The music began and the room exploded with joy. I was overwhelmed with a sense of reverential awe. God was being honored and the worship was absolutely incredible.

I was thrilled to be in such an unforgettable event. Honoring the people at Times Square Church was easy because it was apparent how much they honored the Lord! So for worship to work there are two critical principles from this checkpoint. First, love God with all your heart and honor Him. When you do so it should not be so difficult to honor those (your co-worshipers) who honor Him too!

Debrief with God – *Read John 10*

- What are some ways God is becoming too common in your life?

  _____

  _____

  _____

- What steps can you take to restore your view of God?

  _____

  _____

  _____

- What co-worshiper relationship needs attention in your life right now?

  _____

  _____

  _____

- What should the attention look like and when does it need to happen?

  _____

  _____

  _____

- How can you encourage the spiritual leaders at your church this week?

  _____

  _____

  _____

• How can you express what God has said in a prayer to Him?

_____

_____

_____

DAY 24 – WORSHIP CHECKPOINTS 4-5

O LORD, I call upon You; hasten to me! Give ear to my voice when I call to You!
May my prayer be counted as incense before You;
The lifting up of my hands as the evening offering.
(Psalm 141:1-2)

June Burnette was my wife, Andrea's, grandmother. She was 92-years-old when she went to Heaven. June was the most consistent Christian I have ever known. She was the faithful wife of an Army chaplain and pastor. She served faithfully beside her husband until his death. Up until the last year of her life she served as a greeter at our church. She was an amazing lady who was a teacher, pilot, and a three time all-state basketball player.

What most folks did not know about June was her prayer closet. She always had a place, an actual prayer closet, she visited every morning. She prayed for everyone on her list starting with her family and then her extended family. June read through the Bible twice every year.

June had a consistent walk with God. One of the things I miss most about her was how she always replied to anyone who asked how she was doing. June always answered; *I'm walking in faith and victory.* For me, I feel being consistent is a miracle. But I know God is willing to perform this miracle in my life every day.

Checkpoint #4: **Consistency.** The fourth worship checkpoint is *consistency.* A person who *swears to his own hurt and does not change* (Psalm 15:4) is ready to go deeper in worship with Jesus. This person is careful to keep their promises no matter how difficult that may be. Integrity was the first worship checkpoint. Consistency is a measure of wholeness and a part of our integrity. Consistency can only come from God's power in us. I do what I say because what I say is a reflection of my heart.

Each time we worship God should build on the last time we worshiped Him. We get to know Christ better through authentic worship. If every time we meet with Jesus it is like meeting Him for the first time, then our worship is shallow. Certainly our emotions and circumstances will vary. But God wants worshipers that approach Him regardless of their emotions or personal circumstances. Consistent worship builds consistent believers. In our darkest hour we can find peace through worshiping God.

One of the meanings of the Hebrew word for truth is "absolute consistency." Part of the battle we fight as believers is being consistent in our thoughts, behaviors and attitudes. True worship is a spiritual discipline, so at times the biggest battle is engaging God on a consistent basis. Being consistent, however, is not being perfect but is about an ongoing walk with God. Our public and private personas are in rhythm with God's leadership.

Doing this study and following hard after God for 30 days on a consistent basis is huge. But embracing a new plan 100 days after will be a reflection of what God does in your heart the first 30! Jesus has once again set the standard: "Jesus Christ is the same yesterday and today, yes and forever" (Hebrews 13:8).

We can relate to the apostle Paul all too well in Romans 7. Our lives with God can tend to look like the stock market with wild up and down swings. Right when we think we are making progress then a dramatic dip takes our breath away. Paul confessed, "For I know that nothing good dwells in me, that is, in my flesh; for the willing is present in me, but the doing of the good is not. For the good that I want, I do not do, but I practice the very evil that I do not want" (Romans 7:18-19). Yet God is calling us to grow to a point of greater consistency with Him and other people. Paul expressed his only hope for this consistency was in Christ.

Checkpoint #5: **Stewardship.** The final worship checkpoint, *stewardship*, might be the most personal. All the other checkpoints we can embrace and take next steps. But use of time and money is usually an awkward discussion. Psalm 15:5 described the prepared worshiper as a person *who does not put out his money at interest nor does he take a bribe against the innocent.*

God does not want us to be greedy. All your resources (money, time, talent, assets) are gifts from God to be managed for Him with integrity. The two big ideas about resource management in this passage are:

- *Live by a set of standards with the resources you have.*
- *Do not take or use resources in an unethical manner.*

Another way to understand the idea of steward is as a *manager of the owner's resources.* From a management perspective consider your life a business from God. God is the source and resource for all you are and have. Since all you have belongs to Him you are faithful to serve, steward and invest it for His glory.

You are a small business owner (although it may feel bigger) who makes decisions everyday about how you are going to operate. A business owner (your life) has to decide what the bottom line is in order to live accordingly. So, how's business? How are you managing your time, talents, money, and relationships for the bottom line purpose God has for your life?

This passage has a promise attached to the prepared worshiper: "He who does these things will never be shaken" (Psalm 15:5). Now that is a place where I want to live. My worship life also moves me off the shaky ground of an unexamined life. As I connect with God as a true worshiper not only am I standing on holy ground but solid ground!

Debrief with God - *Read Hebrews 13*

- What area in your life is the most consistent?

  _____

  _____

  _____

- What area in your life is the least consistent?

  _____

  _____

  _____

- Who/what can you help grow in the area of your greatest consistency?

  _____

  _____

  _____

- Who/what can help you grow in your areas of greatest inconsistency?

  _____

  _____

  _____

- How can you use your material resources to encourage someone this week?

  _____

  _____

  _____

- How can you express what God has said in a prayer to Him?

  _____

  _____

  _____

DAY 25 – HOW GOD CHANGES US

Praise the Lord! Sing to the Lord a new song,
And His praise in the congregation of the godly ones.
(Psalm 149:1)

Community Bible Church met in a shopping strip back in the '90s. One Monday afternoon when I was coming out of the office I saw a young lady (later I learned her name was Michelle) trying to get into the building. As I approached her she asked me, "Can I get in that room?"

"Why, did you lose something?" I asked.

"No, I just need to get into that room, I don't know why. But my life is a mess and every time I am in that room something happens to me."

I explained to her that when people begin to praise God His presence enters that place. I invited her into my office and at that point she prayed and asked Christ into her life. Michelle is still an active member of CBC. Although she may not have known the God to whom we were giving praise when she first came to CBC, she had experienced His presence.

The greater work of God is unleashed in the lives of those who worship Him. Michelle had experienced something real about God. God grabbed her attention as someone worth getting to know. Our world is full of people like her who are thirsty for God. People are searching for a God who is alive, that they can taste, touch, and see. But unfortunately many of us live like He is dead. The vision of the *WYW* project started with a series of questions:

- What would it look like if a group of people set aside 30 days to go deeper with God through worship? **[Invite]**
- What would God do in the lives of those worshipers? **[Transform]**
- What would God do in the churches, homes, and communities of those worshipers? **[Send]**

So, does God give anything to those who worship Him? If we come to worship God only to get something back from Him we miss the point. God is not our benevolent father in heaven who spoils us by always saying yes. But you know what? If you really looked closely over your last year you would see that He says *Yes* to us most of the time, even when we don't bother to ask. He loves us so much that He gives us what we need, not merely what we want.

God invites us to a relationship with Him, and *Worship is loving God*. When we worship we show affection and admiration to the God we love. We worship Him because He alone is worthy of our worship. However, there is more.

Worship is not only us loving God but also God loving us. When we move to the place of worship we move to the place of blessing:

- We bless God - *I will bless the Lord at all times* (Psalm 34:1).
- God blesses us - *He is a rewarder of those who seek Him* (Hebrews 11:6).

I am not suggesting lather, rinse and repeat formula in order for you to get something from God you don't need. Lather, rinse and repeat works more for some of us than for others. Some of my hair has turned gray over the years and a bunch of it has just turned loose! But we do love instructions and formulas, don't we? We want something that works for us with minimal effort and guaranteed results.

The same applies to our lives with God. Often we worship with this agenda: *Give me a formula or steps to follow. I want to know God; give me a path. I need God's help; how do I get it?* A more honest way to say this would be: *Give me a bottle to rub so a genie will come out and grant me three wishes to make my life work better.* Our human nature has an appetite for simple instructions and low commitment with over the top results.

God is not bound to a series of rules, regulations and formulas created by His spoiled children. True worshipers do not have a self-centered agenda. They love Him with passion and seek the reality of His presence. True worship is not motivated by the desire for a better or a happier life. Yet the Biblical evidence is clear. God delivers His best to those who truly worship Him!

Debrief with God – *Read Psalm 34*

- How has God blessed you in the past week?

  _____

  _____

  _____

- Who could you encourage by telling your *blessing* story?

  _____

  _____

  _____

- What has been your best time with God lately?

  _____

  _____

  _____

- What is He asking you to do now?

  _____

  _____

  _____

- How have you grown as a worshiper in the past month?

  _____

  _____

  _____

- How can you express what God has said in a prayer to Him?

  _____

  _____

  _____

DAY 26 – GOD IS HERE

Praise the LORD! For it is good to sing praises to our God;
For it is pleasant and praise is becoming.
(Psalm 147:1)

Elijah's confrontation with 450 prophets of Baal (1 Kings 18) provides some strong lessons about the presence of God and worship. Elijah knew a God who was already on top of that mountain. There was no question in His mind about who God was or where He lived. How else can you explain the insanity that would confront 450 pagan prophets single-handedly?

Elijah was determined to prove a point to the people about whose god was real. A burning bull contest was proposed. Both Baal's prophets and Elijah would ask their god to send fire to burn a bull placed on an altar. The real god would answer with fire for everyone to see. Contest over.

The prophets of Baal went first and acted like Christians do at times. They felt incredible pressure to *produce* their god. Read the amazing story (1 Kings 18:21-40) in your scripture assignment today to get the full impact. After some failed attempts at getting Baal to show up they took their rants to another level, "So they cried with a loud voice and cut themselves according to their custom with swords and lances until the blood gushed out on them" (1 Kings 18:28). Yet no matter how hard they tried they could not produce their god.

Elijah talked to the real God who was on Mount Carmel before the crowds arrived. He did not seem worried although he faced incredible odds. He knew the equation: One + God = a majority! He did not invite God to come to Mount Carmel but spoke to Him with calm and confidence because Elijah knew God was already there. And God responded, "Then the fire of the Lord fell…" (1 Kings 18:38).

When I moved to San Antonio in 1988, I had my moments of feeling outnumbered and insignificant. I felt the Lord wanted to me to stand in the center of the city and claim the city for Christ. I took a group of worshipers to Alamo Plaza every Thursday to sing and share the Gospel. We would talk to the vendors, tourists and sometimes locals from the inner city but we seldom had significant crowds.

One Thursday, in spite of the fact that we had no audience, I felt compelled to worship. We sang for about 30 minutes and then I felt compelled from God to preach the Gospel. I thought, *Lord, do you see that no one is here? I feel pretty foolish standing here preaching the Gospel to nobody.* But I did it anyway. I only saw two street vendors in the crowd and I knew that they were already Christians. I went all the way to the end and invited whoever was listening to pray the sinner's prayer. To my knowledge no one who needed to hear was listening.

November of that year I got a phone call from my friend, Phil Waldrep, an evangelist from Alabama. The most unusual thing happened. Phil knew I was at the Alamo Plaza all summer every week. He told me when he had preached the previous evening a young lady came forward at the end of the service. He asked her if she came forward to accept Christ. She answered, "No I did that already in San Antonio this summer. I was waiting for a cab at the Menger Hotel (behind where I sang at Alamo Plaza). I heard a man share the gospel. Right there I gave my heart to Jesus. I was going to go tell him but I rushed to call my mother because she had been praying for me for years."

Like Elijah, I knew that God had sent me to declare His name in San Antonio in spite of being outnumbered. Praise happens because Jesus is already in the room and at work. We don't have to invite Him although we may need to welcome Him. This truth can really make a difference in the way you worship God. We engage His presence when we praise Him. When we praise Him, He moves. He does something that causes people to move from where they are to some place new. He speaks and asks us to speak.

Our desire for God's best can cause an unintended and undesirable result. We try to make Him show up and manufacture His presence to make ourselves feel better. Not only is this counterfeit worship for the worshiper (a waste of time) but a terrible testimony to people outside of Christ (a wasted testimony). We praise God to know Him and to embrace the God who is already in the room!

Debrief with God – *Read 1 Kings 18*

• When do you feel most distant from God?

_____

_____

_____

• What scripture or truth from God could help? (Write out the scripture below)

_____

_____

_____

• When do you feel the most intimidated as a Christ follower?

_____

_____

_____

• What scripture or truth might help? (Write out the scripture below)

_____

_____

_____

• How can you encourage someone who serves your city this week?

_____

_____

_____

• How can you express what God has said in a prayer to Him?

_____

_____

_____

DAY 27 – POINTING TO HEAVEN

Praise the LORD! Praise God in His sanctuary;
Praise Him in His mighty expanse.
Praise Him for His mighty deeds;
Praise Him according to His excellent greatness.
(Psalm 150:1-2)

Do you ever sense a slight contradiction in all of this talk about worship? When we describe God we say He is everywhere, right? The Psalmist (139:7) asked the famous question, "Where can I flee from your presence?" The question is followed by a list of options (Heaven and Hell to name a few).

The greatness of God is seen in this incredible passage. The conclusion: *there is no such place where God is not.* Nowhere does a place exist that He is not already there! He is the God who is *with us.*

So, now we come back to what we say about worship. We talk about *coming before His presence with thanksgiving* (Psalm 95:2) and God being *enthroned upon the praises of Israel* (Ps. 22:3). We enjoy the presence of God and practice the presence of God. First, there is the promise: "Lo, I am with you always" (Matt. 28:20). Therefore, the presence of God is everywhere. Then, there is the experienced, desired, powerful presence of God in worship.

Maybe this example will help. You don't have to be around me very long to hear me talk about my wife. If I started listing what I love and admire about her your 30 days would become longer than you probably hoped for. We were married on May 11, 1991. From that moment we were married every day, every month, and every year since. But unfortunately I am not always in her presence experiencing, in real time, the joy of our relationship. We are always together but not always in the same room.

I would like to say (this would sound really romantic and even weird to some of you) that I think of her every waking moment. But my mind is not that big. Sometimes I focus on other projects or responsibilities. Sometimes I am all into my sons or my grandchildren. But that does not mean my marriage is temporarily dissolved or that my wife no longer exists. We are still connected. At times she is in the room but we are not connected. Then she speaks to me and I am keenly aware of her beauty and sweetness. Her presence becomes real and precious to me.

In a much greater sense (human analogies are limited) God is a part of our world. He lives in every room and every place on the planet. I have an eternal relationship with Him that will never change. This is one truth about the greatness of God that is bigger than I can wrap my brain around. But I believe it without question. I am glad I can believe, without fully understanding, that God is everywhere all the time.

God is in this very room and yet I may or may not be connected to Him. Remember, we defined worship as *loving God*. When I abruptly stop what I am doing to love Him, I experience His presence. I enjoy Him, hear His voice and see His beauty. That is His gift to me!

What is in worship for me? That sounds like a terribly selfish question. A better question is, "How does God glorify Himself in my life through worship?" What God does in response to our praise, prayer, and worship may benefit us but it will ultimately draw attention to Him. God is not feeling neglected. But He loves the world and wants people to know Him. So God would never bless you for you but God would at any time bless you for Him.

God invites us to worship Him; He transforms us when we accept the invitation and then He sends us as a living invitation to others for life with Him. Paul described the work of God that is the foundation for *Will You Worship?*: "But we all, with unveiled face, beholding as in a mirror the glory of the Lord, are being transformed into the same image from glory to glory, just as from the Lord, the Spirit" (2 Corinthians 3:18).

Nothing else matters for God beyond our own personal transformation into someone distinctly different than the world has ever seen. Our caring for mankind or donations to worthy causes makes us no different than other good people worldwide. But the more time we spend with Jesus the more we will look like Him and that is something beautiful to behold. We see an example when God used ordinary disciples to do extraordinary things for Him in Acts: "Now as they observed the confidence of Peter and John and understood that they were uneducated and untrained men, they were amazed, and began to recognize them as having been with Jesus" (Acts 4:13).

Have you ever watched a football game and seen a player point to heaven after he scored a touchdown or made a great play? Although we don't know how sincere he is, he does set a good example of how a believer should praise God. Praise is unashamedly pointing to heaven for the world to see who is really making things happen in my life. Glory to God! May He get all the benefit from my praise!

Debrief with God – *Read Psalm 95*

• What is really going on inside you now?

_____

_____

_____

• How can you change your approach to praising God?

_____

_____

_____

• How can your growth as a worshiper become a positive to those around you?

_____

_____

_____

• What is essential to your continued growth?

_____

_____

_____

• How can you express what God has said in a prayer to Him?

_____

_____

_____

DAY 28 – GOD MOVES ME

Every day I will bless You,
And I will praise Your name forever and ever.
Great is the LORD, and highly to be praised,
And His greatness is unsearchable.
(Psalm 145: 2-3)

When our son, Benjamin, was a preschooler our ministry included a lot of traveling. He traveled with us to every venue. During the mornings when he first woke up, we turned on upbeat worship songs. We danced down the hallways of our house laughing, having fun and enjoying God.

Once we were leading worship for a traditional county seat church in Alabama and the people were not responding well. On the third night of the meeting we opened the service with one of our *dancing down the halls songs*. Benjamin began to dance down the aisle and made his way to the front of the church just having fun.

All of the people in this church were politely embarrassed for us when the song ended. But we had a God moment as a result. I told the people that this is how we acted at home and they should not be embarrassed but rather join in the celebration. God turned that meeting around with the dancing of a four-year old child.

The prophet Isaiah delivered some powerful truth from God to an oppressed people in Isaiah 61. The anxiety level at this time was high with God's people. They were on their way back to their homeland. Babylon, their despised captors, had been overthrown.

God's people were released prisoners. But as much as they had dreamed of going home again their lives were far from perfect. Life was difficult because they had sinned against God. Sin has consequences and depending on which sin some consequences last a lifetime. Also, as this large group went back to Jerusalem the people who had never left did not welcome them home. Conflict was waiting to greet them. Life was still hard. They had been gone for at least 70 years. In the midst of their pain God delivered a word to them through His prophet:

The Spirit of the Lord GOD is upon me, Because the LORD has anointed me To bring good news to the afflicted; He has sent me to bind up the brokenhearted, To proclaim liberty to captives And freedom to prisoners; To proclaim the favorable year of the LORD And the day of vengeance of our God; To comfort all who mourn, To grant those who mourn in Zion, Giving them a garland instead of ashes, The oil of gladness instead of mourning, The mantle of praise instead of a spirit of fainting. So they will be called oaks of righteousness, The planting of the LORD, that He may be glorified. (Isaiah 61:1-3)

The word picture in Isaiah 61:3 is striking. The prophet became an instrument of God to reposition those who are sad by giving them, absolutely free, new clothes. The Spirit of the Lord upon the leader changed the wardrobe of hurting people. (Jesus used this passage and identified Himself as the ultimate fulfillment of this word in Luke 4:18-19.)

Two common life experiences (weddings, funerals) were contrasted to make an important point. Beauty, gladness, and praise are the new, Jesus-given wardrobe like clothes at a wedding celebration. Ashes, mourning, and heaviness are the old wardrobe, like the clothes worn to a funeral. The quick summation: *the Spirit of Jesus changes funerals into weddings!*

One of my church members at CBC fought a long battle with cancer. At the end of her life, when it was apparent that she was not going to get well, we had an unforgettable conversation. She said, "My service cannot be like a regular funeral. Heaven is my reward and I want the people to celebrate with me." She helped plan an unforgettable service of worship and celebration. Her funeral included a 30-minute celebration of praise to the Lord. His presence so filled the room that even the unbelievers walked out with hope. The funeral became a wedding celebration of the eternal relationship between Jesus and one of His precious children. Our sadness dissolved and our focus was on the goodness of God and what He had for our future.

Debrief with God - *Read Isaiah 61*

- What do you have to celebrate in your life with Christ today?

  _____

  _____

  _____

- What are you grieving about now?

  _____

  _____

  _____

- What/Who has helped you overcome grief in the past?

  _____

  _____

  _____

- Who can you encourage that has lost something or someone in the past year?

  _____

  _____

  _____

- How do you want people to remember you in the years to come?

  _____

  _____

  _____

• How can you express what God has said in a prayer to Him?

_____

_____

_____

DAY 29 - GOD DELIVERS ME

I call upon the LORD, who is worthy to be praised,
And I am saved from my enemies.
(Psalm 18:3)

El Salvador has been my destination for numerous mission trips over the years. I have experienced the power of God there in unforgettable ways. One trip took us to a small colony called Calvary in the capital city of San Salvador. We anticipated a great response to the Gospel through an outdoor concert and showing of the *Jesus* movie.

Communist guerillas in the area, upset about the meeting, were determined to cause a blackout. We set up our sound system using portable generators for power. As I began to sing four pole bombs went off causing a blackout in the entire colony. But instead of driving people away, the blackout brought everybody outside to hear the music and watch the *Jesus* movie. Thousands of people heard the Gospel that night and the plan of the enemy was foiled.

How many battles are you fighting on your own today? We have all felt the pressure of Satanic opposition in our lives even though we may not have recognized Satan's involvement. Worship is the place where I recognize Satanic opposition and take my battles to the Lord. The Commander in Chief has never lost a battle; so worship reminds me that God will win.

God's people were about to be confronted by a powerful army. Fear and tension were high but God intervened. He specifically instructed His people to enter into conventional warfare with unconventional weapons. King Jehoshaphat cried out to God in terror: "O our God, will You not judge them? For we are powerless before this great multitude who are coming against us; nor do we know what to do, but our eyes are on You" (2 Chronicles 20:12).

True worship and faith are interwoven principles. Worship is a demonstration of our faith in God and our lack of faith in us. Did you see that mindset in Jehoshaphat's prayer? In fact, a dramatic picture of helplessness is seen when the entire nation including infants, wives, and children stood before God as the King prayed.

God responded with a word though His worship leader, not a prophet! Jahaziel, the worship leader, had a life-changing word from God, "Do not fear or be dismayed because of this great multitude, for the battle is not yours but God's" (2 Chronicles 20:15). Talk about a *wow moment*. The Word and worship are interwoven practices. As God's character and will are revealed in His Word our impulse is to worship Him.

God gave a word that increased the faith of a trembling nation. As their faith increased their worship life became more active. The presence and power of God was more real to them than the presence of their enemies. And their God would ultimately win!

God's people enjoyed His presence through worship. They loved God and God loved them back. Notice the end of this battle and the final defeat of a long standing Moabite enemy: "When they began singing and praising, the LORD set ambushes against the sons of Ammon, Moab and Mount Seir, who had come against Judah; so they were routed" (2 Chronicles 20:22).

My oldest son, David, traveled with me on ministry road trips when he was a boy. On one of those trips I was doing a concert in a small church in Leesville, Louisiana. During the concert I began to sing an old song called, *Praise the Lord*. At the beginning of the second verse I sang, *Now Satan is a liar and he wants to make us think that we are paupers when he knows that we are children of the King*. At that moment a man on the second row began to convulse and cause a terrible disruption. David, seated directly in front of him, turned around to see what was happening. Then he immediately turned back around and refocused on the music.

Several men took this troubled man out of the room. I finished the music, gave my gospel presentation, and ended the service. One of the leaders in the church asked me if I could come to the pastor's office. When I got there the pastor was a little frazzled. He told me that he thought the man was demon possessed.

A little skeptical, I asked him why he thought the man was possessed. He took his Bible and walked behind the man as he began to convulse. Now I was scared and did not know what to do. The pastor began to read the story of Jesus and the demoniac.

He turned to the man and said, "What is your name?"

The demon spoke back and then the pastor spoke to the demon and said, "In the name Of Jesus come out."

The demon screamed and left the man. Then another demon spirit spoke to me and said, "I tried to enter your oldest son but the hand of God was on him." The pastor addressed that demon and the demon was cast out.

The man then received Christ and was dramatically changed. He went on to marry the pastor's daughter and eventually became a minister himself. I left that night understanding the realities of Satanic opposition. Even better I saw that the opposition was no match for the power of God. I learned that day that some battles were way too big to ever consider fighting them alone.

Debrief with God - *Read 2 Chronicles 20*

- What is your greatest source of opposition right now?

_____

_____

_____

- What role is Satan playing in your opposition?

_____

_____

_____

- How can worship, faith and prayer become a more active part of your response?

_____

_____

_____

- What is your favorite story of God's power from your past?

_____

_____

_____

- How can you express what God has said in a prayer to Him?

_____

_____

_____

DAY 30 - GOD FREES ME

So Jesus was saying to those Jews who had believed Him,
If you continue in My word,
then you are truly disciples of Mine;
and you will know the truth, and the truth will make you free.
(John 8:31-32)

A stick displayed in my office reminds me of another El Salvador story. When people ask about it I always tell them that the stick was the greatest love offering I ever received. One day I was singing in an outdoor concert in the central market place of San Salvador. As I was singing in my typical bad Spanish I noticed a homeless man pushing through the crowd to get closer to me. He had no shoes and his clothing was badly worn. He was obviously under the influence of alcohol.

The translators tried to stop him but he was persistent and begged loudly for help. Eventually he grabbed hold of me in the middle of a song and threw up at my feet. I kept singing while some of our men took him, fed him, cleaned him up and prayed for him.

As the worship continued they shared the Gospel and led this homeless man to faith in Christ. I went back to the place where these men were ministering to him and found him sober and in his right mind. He was rejoicing over his new found faith.

A few minutes later as he walked by me to say goodbye I reached in my backpack and gave him a New Testament. He felt such gratitude that he reached into his back pocket and gave me his stick. He told me, "This is the only thing I have but I want you to have it." He left free from the bondage of alcohol and a life of failure. When I returned to the country a year later he met me with the greeting party clean and nicely dressed. He told his story about how God used the worship to call him forward to set him free.

Some people are much more comfortable whistling their way through the graveyard as opposed to confronting their fear and bondage. Worship gatherings can provide temporary relief from life's ailments and challenges. Research confirms that church makes people healthier and happier.

Music has a therapeutic effect on people. Most of you are probably aware of the use of music even in non-religious settings to help people. Music therapy is a professional discipline used to help people with stress, pain management and emotional wellness. Negro spirituals gave African slaves a way to express their faith and hope in God under circumstances more horrific than we could imagine. As they worked in the fields and gathered in their churches they would sing classics, like *Swing Low, Sweet Chariot*. They dreamed about freedom in their current life as well as in Heaven after they died!

Music had a therapeutic and spiritual effect on King Saul. David was appointed an armor bearer to the King. As part of his role, David was music therapist, worship leader, and the deliverer of some spiritual classics from the Psalms. The Bible describes his positive influence on King Saul, "David would take the harp and play it with his hand; and Saul would be refreshed and be well" (1 Samuel 16:23).

Yet we know there is another level of worship beyond better feelings about our current problems. God reveals Himself and His will through worship. He moves people to new levels of obedience. God ultimately makes eternal, transformational changes in the lives of people who worship Him. Music is often a part of that worship and a sign of being set free spiritually.

In the '80s the Louisiana State Penitentiary in Angola was the worst prison in the country. At least 93% of the inmates were in for life and Angola had the distinction as the most violent prison in America. In 1995, Burl Cain became the new warden. He believed that the answer to the violent crime was to bring Christ into the prison. Religious life became a part of the prison life with singers, preachers, and other Christian ministries given the freedom to minister to inmates.

I made 20 trips to the prison over the years. On one trip we were late because we were delayed going through the security process. When we got to the meeting the inmates were already there singing. We set up our gear and began to play. To my amazement the inmate's voices were louder than our guitars, drums and amplified voices combined. To watch those men, who will never get out of prison, sing in complete freedom from their personal bondages was an unforgettable picture. I saw another example of John 8:36, "So if the Son sets you **free**, you will be **free indeed**" lived out in front of me.

A seminary eventually was welcomed to the prison. Every week Bible professors poured life into men who felt a calling from God to be ministers. Now every cell block has a trained pastor. Some of these men transferred to start faith-based programs at the other prisons.

God wants to set you free for your good and His glory. Bondage is the beginning point of a God story in your life. Satan wants you to believe that your bondage is the end of your life. Looking to Jesus through worship and by faith is the place to start. When God really shows up, He shakes places! When He shakes places, He shakes people and breaks chains! That is the God that people are looking for today.

God frees us from bondage – those hurts, habits, and hang-ups that block His best from our lives. Do you want to find God at work? Find out where people are worshiping in spirit and in truth. There you will find this God. At that place He will free you!

Debrief with God – *Read 1 Samuel 16*

- What sin in your life do you need the power of Jesus Christ to help you overcome?

  _____

  _____

  _____

- How can you be more engaged in your city serving people who are hurting?

  _____

  _____

  _____

- How can you pray more intentionally for specific needs in your community?

  _____

  _____

  _____

- Where can you learn about opportunities to take the Gospel to the nations?

  _____

  _____

  _____

- How can you be more involved in praying, giving, and going to the nations?

  _____

  _____

  _____

- How can you express what God has said in a prayer to Him?

  _____

  _____

  _____

Epilogue
The Next 100 Days
What are Your Next Steps?

So then, my beloved, just as you have always obeyed, not as in my presence only, but now much more in my absence, work out your salvation with fear and trembling; for it is God who is at work in you, both to will and to work for His good pleasure.
(Philippians 2:12-13)

Evan Roberts had been dreaming about big things for God since he was a boy. His mining town was famous for all the wrong reasons. Yet there was always room for one more idealistic dreamer. Roberts preached his most famous message to a small group of 17 young people one evening. He challenged them to put away sin, stop questionable habits, listen to the Holy Spirit, and be brave for Christ. The strong message followed by a serious commitment from the entire group. So what happened after that night?

History tells that in the next seven days his town (Loughor) was changed. But the Evan Roberts' story gets even bigger. In the 60 days following over 70,000 people came to Christ. Six months later a total of 100,000 people were saved. What Evan Roberts did on that October night in 1904 really did matter. Now the famous Welsh revival shows the potential of the power of God. But even more it demonstrates what God really wants in every city.

Roberts had an incredible burden for the people of his city and region long before that night. And the God who is able to do beyond what one could ask or imagine took over the area:

As God answered this burden, even the newspapers published the results. In two months, 70,000 were converted, 85,000 in five months, and more than 100,000 in six months. Judges were presented with white gloves signifying no cases to be tried. Alcoholism was halved. At times hundreds would stand to declare their surrender of Christ as Lord. Restitution was made; gamblers and others normally untouched by the ministry of the church came to Christ. [1]

No question the results of the now famous Welsh Revival of 1904-05 was a *God-thing*. On our best day we could not produce those kinds of results. God used a passionate young preacher with a burden for a city. You don't often find, in any generation, that type of maturity, passion, and commitment in a man so young.

But another element of that great, historic, movement of God will make the challenge more personal. Remember the 17 young people who listened to Evan's message? He asked them to make new commitments in their relationship with God and obviously they followed through.

I heard it said once that everybody makes big commitments in the shower. Few people get out, dry off, get dressed, and go do something about it. I think James captured the heart of the matter:

But prove yourselves doers of the word, and not merely hearers who delude themselves. For if anyone is a hearer of the word and not a doer, he is like a man who looks at his natural face in a mirror; for *once* he has looked at himself and gone away, he has immediately forgotten what kind of person he was. But one who looks intently at the perfect law, the *law* of liberty, and abides by it, not having become a forgetful hearer but an effectual doer, this man will be blessed in what he does. (James 1:22-25)

We hope you had an incredible time with God over the past few weeks. Our prayer is that you experienced your greatest intimacy with Him ever. We all tend to be fast starters and slow finishers. Whether it is cleaning our garage, or focusing on spiritual growth, most of us struggle to finish what we start. How many times have we been stirred, inspired, and encouraged but not changed? Books, conferences, and experiences come and go. *Will You Worship?* is only as good as your follow through.

I (Dino) was coached by a man named Bob Logan. Many of you will never know him but you should. He is a hero of the faith who has helped thousands of church planters and leaders over the years. God used him to make a tremendous impact in my life as my coach and mentor. He asked a lot of hard questions that were gifts from God to me.

On one occasion, I had spent a lot of time and energy planning a training event for leaders in South Carolina. Bob helped me think through the event and what I needed to do to get as many people there as possible. He asked me a question after the event I will never forget: "What is your 100 day plan?" All my energy went into the event. The answer that came to mind when Bob asked his 100 day question was, "I think I will take a really long nap."

He explained I needed to plan 100 days after the event to be sure that people were following through on what they had heard and experienced. That represented a big mindset shift for me.

Making room for things like *WYW Project* takes energy in our busy, crazy lives. Our tendencies will be to take a long nap when finished. But what about the long term? That involves much more thought and planning. Our worship lives are too important to be left to chance; we need to be intentional about our relationship with God.

Here is a reality of the *WYW Project*. If the follow up to your experience is not worth a 100 day plan, then it probably was not worth the time or resources you invested from the beginning. We have prayed since long before this started for more than just a warm experience with Jesus. We want to see every man, woman and child in your city hear and see Jesus through you. Our hearts are to see what happened in Wales in 1904 to be repeated in America!

For God to make our vision a reality the *WYW Project* is not over now but instead is just beginning. Charles Finney once defined revival as the beginning of new obedience. We hope God has made permanent changes in you and your relationship with Him. One sign that He is at work is when you keep moving forward. So, what's next?

The target is spiritual transformation by the power of Jesus Christ. When God gets hold of a person, that person starts doing life differently. His influence for Christ is expanded and God is glorified. He does not forget what he learns about himself in the presence of a holy God. He does something about it! So what are your next steps?

10 Steps - 100 Days

Let us offer you a track to run on. Don't feel you have to follow each of these steps. Use them as a planning guide or create your own steps. The key is that you have a plan that stands the test of action. For example, a goal of wanting to think more about God during the day sounds great, but you need to make it a SMART goal (Specific, Measurable, Attainable, Relevant, and Time Specific). A SMART goal related to thinking about God more might be: *Beginning this Monday, at the beginning of my daily lunch break, I will spend 7 minutes with God reading scripture and praying.*

Make SMART goals. You will not achieve every one of them and may need to adjust them after a trial period. But a SMART goal turns dreams and visions to action. Hopefully the steps below will inspire creativity and be used by God to empower action:

1) *Spend the First 10 Days Planning the Next 90* – You may really think that is silly. I am not suggesting you stop what you are doing in the areas of personal worship, Bible reading and prayer during the next 10 days. Keep doing what you have been doing unless of course that needs to change. But a major reason we don't stay the course is because we refuse to

plan or anticipate obstacles to our goals. We get excited and live based on a *ready, fire, aim* philosophy. The unfortunate result is that we either frustrate people we love with all of our good intentions or we disappoint ourselves.

Answer the following questions in light of your normal schedule:

- *What would it look like for me to take my personal worship life to another level?*
- *What would have to change?*
- *Who will be affected by the changes?*
- *What are the keys to my success?*
- *What are the roadblocks to my success?*
- *Who do I need to talk to about this?*

2) *Use a Calendar to Plan* – What you value and are most likely to do is on your calendar. So, put your worship plan on your calendar or smart phone. Anticipate responsibilities and commitments that might interfere with your life of worship. Be flexible! Normally we are taught that we worship God at the same time in the same place every day. When possible, that is good advice. But you are not a failure if your schedule forces you to worship at different times and places. The important thing is to connect with God through a meeting with Him. Planning ahead will ensure that you can move your meetings with God based on your schedule.

3) *Schedule Worship Time Blocks* – For some of you a time block might be two hours. For others the block may be eight hours. Few of you would be able to spend that much time with God every day. But over a 90-day period how often could you possibly enjoy longer periods of time with God? You will learn so much there and gain momentum for the shorter more frequent times with God.

4) *Study Worship Mentors from the Bible* – The Bible has many examples of great worshipers such as David, Miriam and Mary. By watching them worship they can mentor you and deepen your worship life. Let God speak to you through His word. He loves worship and invites you to meet Him there. Our worship time can be enhanced by watching others worship.

5) *Engage Real Time Worship Mentors* – Who do you know that really seems to worship God? We are not talking about people who know a lot or who stand on platforms . . . necessarily. But we are talking about people you have met on your journey who seem to understand and embrace intimacy with God. Arrange a meeting with them and prepare questions in advance to maximize your time.

6) *Leverage Social Media* – Use tools like Facebook, Twitter, blogs, and other online forums to ask key questions about worship like:

- *What book other than the Bible has impacted your relationship with God the most?*
- *What are your keys to prioritizing and protecting time alone with God?*
- *What lessons have you learned about worship from fellow worshipers?*
- *Who has helped you the most in your worship life? How?*

Tweet your discoveries. Let everyone benefit. Tweet articles about worship that hit the target for you.

7) *Use a Worship Journal* – Buy a journal or use a spiral notebook to start writing things about your worship journey. You may write long letters to God or list bullet points. But, having a central place to collect everything you learn and experience about worship is vital for your growth.

8) *Plan Worship Acts of Service* – Serve your city. Serve your family, neighbors, and friends. There is a difference between serving out of duty and serving as a love gift to God. Serve in secret, bless someone who does not know you, or give a gift anonymously. But focus on this as your way to love God.

Oswald Chambers described an interesting aspect of worship that supports the idea of worship through service:

Worship is giving God the best that He has given you. Be careful what you do with the best you have. Whenever you get a blessing from God, give it back to Him as a love-gift.[2]

How about the next time God gives you something, you pass it on to someone else as an act of love and worship to Him!

9) *Be More Intentional About Sunday Gatherings* – Worshiping with people is Biblical and personal. You can worship God on the lake fishing – I mean it is possible, but not likely. Throughout the Bible small and large groups of people met together for worship. Who can be your worship partners? Your Sunday School class or small group might be a great place to start. If you don't have a smaller group to do life with, start one or find one as part of your plan.

10) *Be Vulnerable* – Maybe the word *accountable* might fit you better. But being vulnerable is something you freely volunteer to be, to another person, with a passion for your growth and God's glory. Being visible is another perspective on accountability. Let people see deeper into your life. Put light on your struggles, questions and failures. Discuss your 100-day plan with them. Be honest about your challenges. Ask for prayer and wise counsel. Calendar, even if by phone or email, every time you intend to connect with them over the next 100 days.

God's Pleasure

We began *WYW* talking about a journey – and now we end encouraging you to continue the journey. Life with God is a process that begins when you meet Him and continues for a lifetime.

Paul's heart for the journey of the Philippian Christians to continue is seen in His letter to them. He had witnessed the incredible work of God in the people he met there. But God's story in their lives was nowhere near over, although Paul knew he would never see them again. In his final words to them He encouraged them to "work out" their "salvation with fear and trembling" (Philippians 2:12).

There is so much more of God than most of us ever experience in our lives. We are not talking about weird, mystical experiences. Maybe a simpler way to say it is there is so much more that God wants to change in us over our lifetimes. He wants to change us beyond what we could ever imagine.

What would give God the most pleasure? To let Him do what He wants in and through us. He does not expect us to take this journey alone. He promises that it is His job to change us. It is our job to let Him. Paul continued: "For it is God who is at work in you, both to will and to work for His good pleasure" (Philippians 2:13).

Are we there yet? Actually none of us are but we are moving forward together and dreaming bigger dreams for God. We want to be part of the next great movement of God in the world. Celebrate God's wins over the past 30 days. The trip may not have been perfect but you moved faster than usual. God has so much over the next 100 days and beyond for His glory and mission. Coach yourself through the questions at the end of this section. Keep moving forward and enjoy the journey with Jesus!

Next Steps for My 100 Day Worship Plan - *10 Key Questions*

1. What time will you set aside for planning over the next 10 days?

_____

_____

2. What calendar or planning tool works best for you?

_____

_____

3. What will your extended worship times look like?

_____

_____

4. Who can you talk to about being your worship mentor?

_____

_____

5. What key questions will you ask them?

_____

_____

6. How can you use the social media (Facebook, Twitter, blogs, etc.) to help?

_____

_____

7. What are your next steps in implementing use of a worship journal?

_____

_____

8. How can you take serving God to another level in your life?

_____

_____

9. How can you get more out of public worship gatherings?

_____

_____

10. What small group do you need to help you grow?

_____

_____

Now write a prayer asking for God's strength, guidance and power to follow through!

_____

_____

Small Group Gatherings – *Will You Worship?*

Six weeks of small group gatherings are a valuable part of the *WYW* process. The material is designed to complement and enhance the DVD's and journal. Further discussion and application of *WYW* principles are critical for living a transforming life. *Application* is allowing God's truth to affect the way that we live. He gets great glory in our cities and communities when our lives are changed by His truth.

Group leaders should think like discipleship coaches not just teachers. A teacher is responsible to *complete the lesson*. A coach sees transformation in the lives of the people he/she coaches as the target! The coach asks great questions and encourages next steps.

The small group agendas are driven by the value of involving people in the conversations. They are open-ended to encourage people to think and make decisions. You will not likely have time to cover all the questions particularly if people are involved. Pick the questions that match your group the best and consider creating a few of your own.

Make sure everyone has at least one *next step* before the small group meeting is over. Check up on the next steps each week you meet. Pray for each other that God would do an incredible transformational work in and around each person in your group (Philippians 2:13).

Gathering #1 – A New Thing (My Ultimate Priority)

Key Word – Space

Big Idea - *God has created us to worship Him.*

God's Story - Isaiah 43:14-21

Talk Back
- What was the best toy you ever had as a child?
- What did you tell people you wanted to be when you grew up?

Introduction
The ultimate priority in your life is to worship God. You were created for that purpose. God wants to do a new thing through your worship life. Other roles, responsibilities, and tasks require energy and attention in your life. But everything starts with worship. From that source many can find life with God through you.

Heart Matters
Worship is not something else to add to an overcrowded life. The reason many sincere people struggle with a worship life is they don't attempt to make space for worship. Worship requires permanent space in your life, not temporary space that is dedicated on a random basis, when time allows. We hope the next 30 days is the beginning of something that lasts forever.

Have you ever said, "My plate is full," to describe your busy life? So, how do you create more space in a life that is already full and running over?

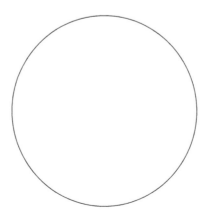

Take a few moments and let your inner artist come out! Draw simple symbols on the picture (stick people work) that represent everything that is currently on your plate. Be creative. But then, take a fearless inventory. Look at all the items.

- What items are *good for you* and what items are not?
- What can possibly be moved off your plate to make more space for God?
- What's missing?
- One year from now how would you like your plate to look different?
- Where does life with God belong?
- What needs to change?

God's Story – Isaiah 43:14-21

God's people in the Old Testament were on an epic adventure with Him. From the time they were slaves in Egypt to their 40 years in the wilderness they experienced many highs and lows. This episode in Isaiah's time was God's presentation of His love and purpose for His people.

Read the passage below by section and briefly discuss the key questions. Moving into groups of two or three people will enhance the discussion time.

An Awesome King-Creator (43:14-15)
- What benefits did God's people enjoy in this story?
- What encourages you the most about belonging to God?

Encouraged by the Past (43:16-17)
- What are some things God had done in the past for His people in this story?
- What are some things God has done in your past?

Focused on the New Thing (43:18-19)
- What unique needs of the people in this story was God going to meet?
- What unique needs in your city/community do you believe God wants to meet?

Making Space for Honor and Praise (43:20-21)
- How does honor and praise make God famous?
- How would a deeper life of worship make a difference in your city/community?

Final Debrief
- What was most important for you to hear in this small group meeting?
- What is one big "next step" you need to take this week?
- Who can help you?

Pray in smaller groups of two or three people that God would help you create space for worship in your life.

Memorable Verse – Isaiah 43:19

Behold, I will do something new,
Now it will spring forth;
Will you not be aware of it?
I will even make a roadway in the wilderness,
Rivers in the desert.

Gathering #2- An Encounter with God (The Worship Cycle)

Key Word - Transform

Big Idea – *God transforms our lives during difficult times through worship and obedience.*

God's Story – Isaiah 6

Talk Back
- What was the hardest job you ever had?
- What lesson(s) did you learn from the work experience?

Introduction
When life goes wrong we tend to withdraw from God and others. We may be angry with God because we think He should not have allowed something bad to happen. Also, people may have disappointed us in the past. Either way we feel unsafe talking about our deepest hurts and fears. Yet God invites us to Him to worship and be comforted during our darkest days. He also provides help through His people.

God uses worship to do His deepest work in our lives. He does his greatest work when we are desperate and in pain. Yet worship is never meant to merely help us feel better about ourselves and our life situations. Worship is to help us see from God's perspective and to learn what He wants us to do next.

Heart Matters
Read the following statement: ***Worship is loving God.***

- What is unique about it?
- How does it help you?
- What's missing in the statement?

Write your own definition of worship. In smaller groups of two or three people read your definitions. Choose the best one to share with the larger group.

God's Story – Isaiah 6
Isaiah is considered the greatest of the Old Testament prophets. His job as God's prophet was hard. God's message through him was not always popular. His world was in turmoil. His friend and king, Uzziah had died after making critical mistakes as a leader. His country was vulnerable to enemies who wanted to take over. Isaiah was walking through

the darkest days of his life. Even in your darkest days God invites you to worship Him. When you meet Him there, He will change you.

Read the passage below by section and briefly discuss the key questions. Moving into groups of two or three people will enhance the discussion time.

Celebrating and Loving God (6:1-4) *Praise and Adoration*
- What lessons do you learn about God in these verses?
- What are the best worship environments for you?

Adjusting My Life to God (6:5-7) *Confession*
- What difficult lessons was Isaiah learning about himself?
- What difficult lessons have you learned about yourself in the last year?

Embracing God's Heart (6:8) *Listening*
- What made God's voice clear in this story?
- When is the last time God spoke clearly to you?

Finding My Place (6:8-13) *Obedience*
- What was hard about what God was asking Isaiah to do?
- What is your biggest challenge to obeying God?

Final Debrief
- What did you need to hear the most from the discussion today?
- What is the biggest challenge in your life right now?
- How can you better prepare to meet that challenge this week?
- Who can help you?

Have each person write their biggest challenge on an index card. Have them pass it to someone else in the group and pray for them each day in the week to come. Pray for each other to have God's strength to face the challenges of the week with worship and obedience.

Memorable Verse – Isaiah 6:8

Then I heard the voice of the Lord, saying,
"Whom shall I send, and who will go for Us?"
Then I said, "Here am I. Send me."

Gathering #3 – Worship is a Verb (Active Worship)

Key Word - Action

Big Idea - *God is the audience of our worship, we are the actors.*

God's Story - Psalm 100

Talk Back
- What is the best vacation you ever had?
- What do you like to do for fun?

Introduction
Worship is not a spectator sport. Our best moments are when we are doing something. Our children are not the only ones who get bored easily. Yet for many reasons we struggle with the *doing* and *acting* part of worship. We love to hear our favorite singers and musicians. But real worship requires our involvement.

Worship is action. A different picture of worship may help. Our hearts and minds must shift from being part of the audience to part of the program. An audience mentality will produce a *"What's in it for me?"* consumer approach to worship. But we are not consumers when we gather. We are the presenters and God is the audience. So, worship is not sitting on the sidelines and rating the performance of others. Worship is being on the program!

Heart Matters
- What does a great worship gathering look like?
- What are your favorite elements of public worship gatherings?
- How can you engage those elements on a deeper level at the next gathering?
- How can you encourage your worship leaders this week?

God's Story – Psalm 100
The Psalms were written because we need worship leadership. We really do want to grow deeper with God in worship. But we often wonder what worship should really look like and why it seems so uncomfortable at times. Rest assured you are not alone. God wrote the longest book in the Bible to help people just like you learn to worship and know Him better!

Psalm 100 is an invitation to actively celebrate the work of God. Some believe it could have celebrated the opening of a new temple. The great thing about this invitation is that it includes instructions about what to do if you accept!

Read the passage below by section and briefly discuss the key questions. Moving into groups of two or three people will enhance the discussion time.

Bring Your Best (100:1-2)

- What is the biggest obstacle to giving your best in public worship?
- What adjustment do you need to make in order to give your best?

Think Relationship (100:3)

- What does it mean to belong to God?
- How can that influence your approach to worship?

Give Praise and Thanks (100:4)

- What are some things you admire about God?
- What has God done in your life over the past month that you appreciate?

Focus on the Big Picture (100:5)

- How would you like your relationship with God to look 5 years from now?
- Who would you like to influence the most for Christ over that time period?

Final Debrief

- What was most important for you to hear in this small group meeting?
- What is one big *next step* you need to take this week?
- Who can help you?
- What kind of progress did you make with last week's next step?

In groups of two or three people, pray with one another that God would give courage and strength to take the next step with Him.

Memorable Verse – Psalm 100:5

For the LORD is good;
His lovingkindness is everlasting
And His faithfulness to all generations.

Gathering #4 – Get Ready to Meet God

Key Word - Preparation

Big Idea - *Preparing to worship is as important as worship.*

God's Story - Psalm 15

Talk Back
- Who was the best neighbor you ever had?
- Who was the strangest neighbor you ever had?

Introduction

When it comes to life with God you can't always have it your way. All you can eat buffet restaurants are quite popular with most people. The thought of going out to eat and getting all you want of exactly what you want is enticing. The same mentality can influence our lives with God. Yet when it comes to going deeper with God getting all you want of exactly what you want does not work well.

Everything about you matters to God. You may love the music or ministries of the church. You may even love the pastor or the special programs. Jesus may be an inspiration to you. But you will never experience the life God intended until you live life on His terms. Simply put that means your approach to people and life will change.

Heart Matters

Oswald Chambers explained his list of priorities this way:

It must be God first, God second, God third, until the life is faced steadily with God and no one else is of any account.[1]

- What do you think Chambers means by that statement?
- What would you add to that statement or take away to make it better?
- What would you need to change to live with those priorities?

God's Story - Psalm 15

Worshiping God is the most important practice of any Christ-follower. Our lives with God flow from the vitality of our worship. Worship is a lifestyle that we agree can be all day, every day. Yet our lives are also marked by intentional time focusing on God and His greatness. We are made to desire and enjoy His presence.

If Almighty God invites us to worship Him we should be honored and humbled. Preparation is essential for anything important. Preparation for worship happens by the way we live. The Psalms were God's gift to people who wanted to experience an authentic relationship with Him. Psalm 15 explains how we should live in order to enjoy a worship life with Him that is real and meaningful. Below are five worship checkpoints to help us align our lives with God's will and prepare for worship.

Read the passages (Psalm 15) below by section and briefly discuss the key statements. Moving into groups of two or three people will enhance the discussion time.

Integrity (15:1-2)

- *I am honest with God and other people about who I am.*

Consideration (15:3-4)

- *I care for people, even those who are not like me.*

Honor (15:3-4)

- *I honor God and my co-worshipers (others who love and worship Him).*

Consistency (15:5)

- *I keep my promises and commitments.*

Stewardship (15:5)

- *I manage time, money, and people as sacred gifts from God.*

Final Debrief
- What was most important for you to hear in this small group meeting?
- What statement of the five statements above best describes you?
- What statement least describes you?
- What area needs the most attention in your life?
- What is one big "next step" you need to take this week?
- What kind of progress did you make with last week's next step?

Pray for each other in groups of two or three people for God to give wisdom and power to live all out for Him.

<u>Memorable Verses – Psalm 15:1-2</u>

O LORD, who may abide in Your tent?
Who may dwell on Your holy hill?
He who walks with integrity, and works righteousness,
And speaks truth in his heart.

Gathering #5 – Worship and Life (God is Here)

Key Word - Invite

Big Idea - Worshiping God invites Him into difficult situations

God's Story – 2 Chronicles 20:13-22; Acts 16:25-34; Job 1:13-22

Talk Back
- Who was the most famous person you ever met?
- What was the most memorable gift you have ever received?

Introduction
True worship is all about God, His purposes, and His ways. Yet there are benefits to the worshiper as well. God responds to the worship and praise of His people. He also gets glory when people draw attention to Him through worship.

The challenges of everyday life often have no obvious or immediate solutions. So, how do we respond to bad circumstances? We have plenty of options. But the best option is to gain God's perspective, power, and presence through worship.

Heart Matters
- What was the biggest win in your life over the past 6 months?
- What is your biggest fear/concern now?
- What is God's perspective on your circumstances?

God's Story
The Bible was written to people in pain. They were people just like us. Success and failure were a part of everyday life for them. Disappointments as well as victories were common. They all had perfectly good reasons at times to feel helpless and afraid.

God was their refuge and strength when they called on Him. When God was present, worship and praise were common. Not only were worship and praise signs of His presence but also signs of His impending deliverance. Worship and praise were tools of God to deliver His peace, courage, and victory.

Review the following passages about God's intervention. If your group is large enough assign a passage to smaller groups to review and discuss the questions. Then invite groups back to share with the entire group their story and discoveries.

Winning Against All Odds (2 Chronicles 20:13-22)
- What was the challenge faced by God's people?
- What were their options?
- How did worship and praise help the situation?
- What lessons can we learn from the story?

Get out of Jail Free (Acts 16:25-34)
- What was the challenge faced by Paul and Silas?
- What were their options?
- How did worship and praise help the situation?
- What lessons can we learn from the story?

Life after Bad News (Job 1:13-22)
- What was the challenge faced by Job?
- What were his options?
- How did worship and praise help the situation?
- What lessons can we learn from the story?

Final Debrief
- Which of the three situations described above are similar to what you are facing now?
- What is the most important lesson that can help you in the next month?
- What can you do as a next step to help you remember and practice what you have learned?

Pray in groups of two or three people that God would give power to respond to life's challenges in a way that would make Him famous and the strength to take next steps.

Memorable Verse – 2 Chronicles 20:17

You need not fight in this battle; station yourselves, stand and see the salvation of the LORD on your behalf, O Judah and Jerusalem. Do not fear or be dismayed; tomorrow go out to face them, for the LORD is with you.

Gathering #6 – Your Next 100 Days (Optional)

Key Word - Continue

Big Idea - *Growing as a worshiper is a lifelong process that requires focus.*

God's Story – Philippians 2:1-18

Talk Back
- What was your favorite thing to do when you were a child?
- What did you "quit" as a child that you wished you would have stuck with?

Introduction
We tend to start fast but finish slow. What causes us to be slow finishers? One reason is we look for instant solutions. The minute we get bored or our results are below expectations we quit to search for something new. Another reason we finish slow is that we live without goals or long-term plans. Great goals and plans anticipate obstacles that can otherwise cause us to give up.

The word "sequel" is most often used to describe a movie that continues the next installment of a continuing story. A Christ-worshiper should always be stretching toward the next part of His story. The *WYW* sequel is all in your hands. What's next for you? What's next for your church and community? The vision for a movement of God will become a reality because thousands of us begin a new worship journey with Jesus that we continue the rest of our lives.

Heart Matters
On the last day of my life I will love Him more deeply and serve Him more effectively than ever. My last day will be my best day for Him!
Read the statement above.

- Pick out the most important word or phrase to you.
- How does this reflect the desire of your heart?
- What would the last day look like for you?
- What changes do you need to make to finish well as a worshiper?

God's Story – Philippians 3:1-18
Paul's letter to the Christ-worshipers of Philippi is believed to be his last. Much of his advice from God involved a view toward continuing and finishing well for Him. In today's

story from Philippians 3 you will discover important changes that will help you continue on your current path as a life-long Christ-worshiper.

Read the passage below by section and briefly discuss the key questions. Moving into groups of two or three people will enhance the discussion time.

A Mindset Shift (2:1-4)
- What does the new mindset look like?
- How does your mindset need to change?

A Focus on Jesus Christ (2:5-11)
- What did Christ's mindset look like?
- How can we live a life that "exalts Him"?

A Passion to Keep Going (2:12-13)
- Who is your spiritual hero or mentor?
- What is your biggest challenge to continue with Jesus?

A Changed Attitude and New Behavior (2:14-18)
- What have you complained about the most over the last month?
- What are some steps you can take to have a more Christ-like attitude?

Final Debrief
- What is your big takeaway from today's story?
- What is one big "next step" you need to take this week?
- How do you need to prepare to take that step?
- Who can help you?

Pray in groups of two or three people that God would give you the power and vision to continue your next steps with Him.

Memorable Verse – Philippians 2:13

For it is God who works in you,
both to will and to work for his good pleasure.

Endnotes

Day 2: The Big Picture
[1]Paul David Tripp, *Instruments in the Redeemer's Hands: People in Need of Change Helping People in Need of Change* (Phillipsburg, New Jersey: P&R Publishing, 2002), p.73.

Day 6: Forever Worship
[1]Dennis Jernigan, *We Will Worship* (Shepherd's Heart Music, Inc., 1989), Reprinted by Permission.

[2]See http://lastdaysministries.org/Articles/1000008653/Last_Days_Ministries /LDM/Discipleship_Teachings/%20%20Keith_Green/Will_You_Be.aspx (Accessed 10/6/2010)

Day 9: Loving Jesus Lavishly
[1]Kenneth E. Bailey, *Jesus Through Middle Eastern Eyes: Cultural Studies in the Gospels* (Downers Grove, IL: IVP Academic, 2008), pp. 246-247.

Day 15: Serve and Sing
[1]Rick Warren, *The Purpose Driven Life: What on Earth Am I Here For?* (Grand Rapids, MI: Zondervan, 2002), pp. 64-65.

Day 17: Enter with Thanks and Praise
[1]William Barclay, *The Daily Bible Series: The Gospel of Luke*, Revised Edition (Philadelphia: The Westminster Press, 1975), p.218.

Day 18: Say Good Things
[1]Kenneth W. Osbeck, *Amazing Grace: 366 Inspiring Hymn Stories for Daily Devotions* (Grand Rapids, MI: Kregel Publications, 1990), p. 274.

Day 19: Are You Ready for Dinner?
[1]See http://www.christianitytoday.com/ch/131christians/innertravelers/brotherlawrence.html (accessed 11/1/2011)

Day 20: Getting Ready To Go
[1]Robert J. Morgan, *Then Sings My Soul Book 2: 150 of the World's Greatest Hymn Stories* (Nashville: Thomas Nelson, 2004), pp. 46-47.

Day 23: Worship Checkpoint 3
[1]Oswald Chambers, *The Complete Works of Oswald Chambers* (Grand Rapids, Michigan: Discovery House Publishers, 2000), p.194.

The Prologue: The Next 100 Days – *What's Next?*
[1]Malcolm McDow and Alvin L Reid *Firefall, How God Shaped History Through Revivals* (Nashville: Broadman-Holman Publishers, 1997), pp. 277-278.

[2]See http://utmost.org/worship/ (accessed 1/24/2011)

Gathering #4 – Get Ready to Meet God
[1]Oswald Chambers, *The Complete Works of Oswald Chambers* (Grand Rapids, Michigan: Discovery House Publishers, 2000), p.194.

More Resources for Your Church or Small Group from *Will You Worship?*

The *Will You Worship?* DVD Series

Featuring Ray Jones, Worship Ministry Pastor teaching before a live audience at Community Bible Church www.communitybible.com. Ray teaches the 5 major themes of WYW in 5 sessions. This resource will make a great supplement for small groups, churches, or individuals who are on the 30-day personal worship journey.

The *Will You Worship?* 30 Day Journal

These journals make great gifts for friends or family and others you are helping in their journey with Christ. Small groups, churches, and leadership teams can also take the journey together.

To order additional journals or the DVD series go to cbcmusicstore.com. For more information email us at wyw@cbcmail.org or call (210) 477-5179

CPSIA information can be obtained at www.ICGtesting.com
Printed in the USA
LVOW02s0724020813

345541LV00006B/421/P